D0024574

AFRICAN AMERICAN ISSUES

**Recent titles in
Contemporary American Ethnic Issues**

Native American Issues
Paul C. Rosier

U.S. Latino Issues
Rodolfo F. Acuña

Asian American Issues
Mary Yu Danico and Franklin Ng

AFRICAN AMERICAN ISSUES

KEVIN D. ROBERTS

Contemporary American Ethnic Issues
Ronald H. Bayor, Series Editor

GREENWOOD PRESS
Westport, Connecticut • London

Library of Congress Cataloging-in-Publication Data

Roberts, Kevin D. (Kevin David), 1974-
  African American issues / Kevin D. Roberts.
      p. cm. — (Contemporary American ethnic issues, ISSN 1543–219X)
  Includes bibliographical references and index.
  ISBN 0–313–33240–1 (alk. paper)
  1. African Americans—Social conditions—1975– 2. United States—Race relations.
3. African Americans—Race identity. 4. Racism—United States. 5. United States—Social
policy—1993– I. Title. II. Series.
  E185.86.R613 2006
  305.896'073—dc22   2005025441

British Library Cataloguing in Publication Data is available.

Library of Congress Catalog Card Number: 2005025441
ISBN: 0–313–33240–1
ISSN: 1543–219X

First published in 2006

Greenwood Press, 88 Post Road West, Westport, CT 06881
An imprint of Greenwood Publishing Group, Inc.
www.greenwood.com

Printed in the United States of America

The paper used in this book complies with the
Permanent Paper Standard issued by the National
Information Standards Organization (Z39.48–1984).

10 9 8 7 6 5 4 3 2 1

for my wife, Michelle

CONTENTS

SERIES FOREWORD

Northern Ireland, the Middle East, and South Asia are just some of the places where ethnic/racial issues have divided communities and countries. The United States has a long history of such division that often has erupted into violent conflict as well. In America, a nation of immigrants with many ethnic and racial groups, it is particularly important to understand the issues that separate us from one another. Nothing could be more damaging to our nation of nations than the misconception of others' opinions on controversial topics.

The purpose of this series is to provide the means by which students particularly, but also teachers and general readers, can comprehend the contentious issues of our times. The diverse groups chosen for inclusion are the country's main ethnic/racial minorities. Therefore, the groups covered are African Americans, Native Americans, Asian Americans, Latino Americans, Jewish Americans, and Muslim Americans. Each book is written by an expert on that group, a scholar able to explain and discuss clearly in a narrative style the points of friction within the minority and between the minority and majority.

Each volume begins with the historical background of a contemporary issue, including court decisions and legislative action, that provides context. This introduction is followed by the pros and cons of the debate, various viewpoints, the opinion of notables, questions for discussion or paper topics, and recommended reading. Readers of this series will become conversant with such topics as affirmative action and reparations, Indian names and images in sports, undocumented immigrants and border control, intermarriage, separation of church and state, old-world ties and assimilation, and racial profiling.

Knowledge about such concerns will help limit conflict, encourage discussion, and clarify the opinions of those who disagree with majority views. It is important, especially for students, to recognize the value of a different point of view.

Also of importance is realizing that some issues transcend ethnic/racial boundaries. For example, stereotypical images are concerns of both Native Americans and Asian Americans, affirmative action and reparations are more than black-white controversies, and separation of church and state affects Muslim as well as Jewish Americans. These subjects are perennial ones in American history and serve to illustrate that they need to be discussed in a way that brings attention to various views.

This type of series would have served a useful purpose during earlier years when Americans searched for answers and clarification for complex issues tied to race and ethnicity. In a nation that has now become more diversified and during a period once again of extensive immigration, it is time to look at our disputes and calmly appraise and discuss.

Ronald H. Bayor
Series Editor

INTRODUCTION

African Americans occupy a unique position in modern American society. Long the largest ethnic minority in the United States, African Americans are now outnumbered by Latinos. As that demographic shift begins to show its social, cultural, and political impact, concerns over black–white relations, discrimination, and racism have seemingly become less significant than questions over immigration, bilingual education, and workers' visas. As one observer has commented, "Black political power and influence ... must be re-conceptualized in the concept of an America that is far more diverse than simply white and black people."[1]

Thus, as a result of the hard-won gains of the civil rights movement, slavery, Jim Crow segregation, and racism—the crucible of the black experience in America—are now fading memories in the minds of many young black Americans. While the progress in diminishing racism during the last four decades is impressive, the loss of memory of those tragic events also poses a practical problem for those black Americans who still seek additional progress: how do they galvanize support among African Americans for such change? In that respect, the old questions of education and employment remain pivotal issues in the path toward full freedom from racism.

Talk with practically any group of black Americans today, and the major problems they see are day-to-day concerns. On the surface, such problems may seem like completely individual or personal concerns. To the contrary, they actually speak to much larger national and institutional issues facing most African Americans. Imprisonment of friends and loved ones, high rates of out-of-wedlock births, poverty, and low graduation rates continue to impact the black people in the United States. Although the group of black Americans with whom one speaks may talk of these concerns in very personal terms—"my son is in jail," "my daughter is pregnant again"—the broad, national aspect of these issues must not be obscured. When viewed through that lens, one can appreciate that these problems are continuities from the past, problems that have not yet been touched by the diminishing prevalence of racism in the United States.

Some African Americans are well aware of this. A recent Gallup poll asked Americans, "How would you describe race relations between blacks and whites?" Approximately 70 percent of whites said "good" or "very good." While nearly 60 percent of blacks said the same, 81 percent of black respondents said that they had experienced some kind of racially motivated discrimination during the previous year.[2] The recognition among most African Americans that the progress made against racism is not total pervades their view on other issues.

Thus, given the continuing high awareness of racism among African Americans, the purpose of this book is to highlight those issues that are both most significant for black Americans today and most illustrative for students trying to understand the historical and contemporary aspects of African American life. Each chapter begins with a vignette that encapsulates the issue at hand, then proceeds to an event or issue that has recently received significant attention. Central to understanding each issue is its historical background, so each chapter includes a section that provides that context. Finally, every chapter culminates in an examination of the competing positions on the issue presented. Because I am interested in bringing the issue to life, I highlight personalities on each side whose actions, writings, or speeches have influenced how the issue is perceived. Having the words of such people helps us to focus on the arguments as well as on their effectiveness.

Chapter 1 is a fitting start to this book, as it covers the controversy over reparations for slavery. Understanding the issue of slavery reparations requires a solid grasp of African American history, so this chapter provides a thorough historical context for slavery that is helpful in developing an appreciation of the issues covered in the subsequent chapters. Moreover, the arguments of both supporters and opponents of reparations echo those made by their counterparts on other issues. Though the controversy over reparations may not possess the practical, day-to-day significance of issues such as imprisonment and affirmative action, it is nonetheless an issue that evokes deeply held emotions by African Americans.

Chapters 2, 3, and 4 examine three issues that have been longstanding questions among, and of, African Americans: imprisonment, cultural assimilation, and affirmative action. Chapter 2 explores the phenomenon of a disproportionately high rate of African Americans serving prison terms. Accusations of racism in the nation's criminal justice system form the basis of calls for reform. Opponents argue, on the other hand, that a disproportionate number of blacks are in prison because a disproportionate number of blacks commit crime. While little common ground exists between the two sides, the issue is helpful in understanding how other issues—such as poverty, family structure, and education—may impact this particular issue. Likewise, the focus of chapter 3, cultural assimilation, examines whether African Americans should make a better attempt to assimilate with America's "melting pot" culture. Supporters of assimilation maintain that black Americans would see many problems diminish if they would commit themselves to cultural conventions such as standard English; opponents argue that developments such as Ebonics and Kwanzaa represent black cultural heritage, and that they should therefore be allowed to continue in the same way in which other ethnic institutions are commonplace. Finally, in switching gears from culture to the law, Chapter 4 examines the issue of affirmative action. Clearly one of the central controversies involving African Americans, the question of affirmative action's continuation has galvanized people on both sides. Supporters argue that continued racism in the country requires the policy to remain in effect, while opponents suggest that affirmative action now does more harm than good. Recent public opinion data point to a growing consensus among African Americans that affirmative action needs tweaking, but a vast majority of African Americans still see it as providing a level playing field and diversity in the workplace.[3]

Chapters 5 and 6 explore two controversies in education: vouchers and standardized tests. These two issues are consistently mentioned by African Americans as central concerns. That sentiment is logical, as the history of public education for African Americans is a relatively recent development, following years of racism and unequal, underfunded black schools. Perceived as the most effective path to better jobs and more stable homes, African Americans, like most Americans, place considerable emphasis on education policy issues. The first of these covered in this book, vouchers, has always received substantial support by African Americans, as the policy allows them to take their children from low-performing schools. Supporters of vouchers therefore see the policy as revolutionary in American public education, particularly in providing access to excellent schools for students who historically have been underprivileged educationally. But opponents express concerns over the draining of resources from public schools, as well as the potential problem of using public resources at private, religiously affiliated schools. The debate over school choice is particularly important to African Americans given the persistent achievement gap between white and black students on standardized tests. The subject of chapter 6, the issue of a possible racial bias in standardized tests, evokes strong emotions among supporters and opponents of the tests. Supporters contend that such tests are crucial to secondary education, especially with the passage of the No Child Left Behind Act of 2002; opponents argue that too much evidence exists of racial and cultural bias for such high-stakes tests to determine grade promotion, college admission, or professional licensure. Underpinning most of the issues explored in this book, the issue of education is a key concern for African Americans.

The final three chapters cover some of the most important hot-button issues in African American life today: welfare reform, black stereotypes, and election reform. Chapter 7 examines the national move toward welfare-to-work laws. Supporters argue that these policies advance the American sentiment of work-for-assistance, while opponents express dismay over the disproportionate number of black Americans affected by the legislation. The debate over welfare reform involves a considerable amount of black stereotypes, which chapter 8 explores. Sifting through the subtle yet powerful ways that African Americans are stereotyped in modern U.S. society, the chapter highlights those who support stereotypes as reflecting reality, as well as those who oppose any stereotyping at all. Finally, in what may be the single most important concern for African American leaders today, election reform is the focus of chapter 9. Using the 2000 election controversy as a starting point, the chapter examines the long history of voter discrimination and intimidation against African Americans and attempts to place in context the specific concerns of black voters in 2000 and 2004. Supporters of election reform argue for updated voting technology and for a full commitment by the federal government for evenly enforced registration guidelines. Opponents of election reform argue that concern is exaggerated, and even invented, in an attempt to galvanize political support.

Thus, the nine chapters of this book cover the most significant issues facing African Americans today. When I began this project, I had hoped to write a book that brought to life the most salient issues, activists, and ideas in African American life today. The discussion questions that follow each chapter are designed to elicit critical thinking, evoke spirited debate, and spur you to a thorough understanding of African American issues. What follows, then, is a roadmap into that world.

NOTES

1. Joe Hicks, "The Changing Face of America," *Los Angeles Times,* 20 July 1997.
2. "81 Percent of Blacks Face Discrimination: Poll," *Chicago Sun-Times,* 29 August 2003.

3. Black America's Political Action Committee, Annual Opinion Poll, 2003, http://www.bampac.org/opinion_polls2003.asp.

SUGGESTED READING

Dyson, Michael. *Race Rules: Navigating the Color Line.* New York: Vintage, 1997.

Franklin, John Hope. *The Color Line: Legacy for the Twenty-First Century.* Columbia: University of Missouri Press, 1993.

Franklin, John Hope, and Alfred A. Moss, Jr. *From Slavery to Freedom: A History of African Americans.* New York: Alfred A. Knopf, 2000.

Gates, Henry Louis, Jr., and Cornel West. *The Future of the Race.* New York: Alfred A. Knopf, 1996.

Horton, James Oliver, and Lois E. Horton. *Hard Road to Freedom: The Story of African America.* New Brunswick, N.J.: Rutgers University Press, 2001.

West, Cornel. *Race Matters.* New York: Vintage, 1994.

Williams, Lea E. *Servants of the People: The 1960s Legacy of African American Leadership.* New York: St. Martin's Press, 1998.

1

•◦•◦•

SLAVERY REPARATIONS

Few issues in the United States ignite controversy as consistently as the historical legacy of slavery. Abolished well over a century ago, slavery continues to serve as a lightning rod for political interest groups on both sides of the American political spectrum, as well as for individuals whose ancestors were involved in slavery—either as slaveholders or as slaves. The most consternating aspect of the debate that rages over slavery's legacy is the relatively recent efforts to seek reparations, or financial payments, for slavery. Those people leading such efforts, which come in the form of lawsuits and federal government action, argue that slavery's long-term legacy has been wholly negative for the ancestors of slaves, African Americans. The opposing viewpoint, which challenges the call for reparations in both the courtroom and in Congress, argues that the issue of slavery reparations does more to perpetuate long-standing racial problems than to help heal such tensions. As each side raises its rhetoric, the question of reparations becomes a proxy debate for the status of modern race relations in the United States.

H.R. 40

Every year since 1989, Congressman John Conyers (D-MI) has authored and submitted House Resolution 40, which principally aims to establish a committee to investigate the plausibility of making reparations. Observing that "the question of reparations for African Americans remains unresolved," Conyers concludes that Americans "must talk about slavery and its continued

Rohulamin Quander, a descendant of one of George Washington's slaves, sits on the porch of Mount Vernon, Washington's estate in Mount Vernon, Virginia, in 2001 (AP Wide World Photo/Linda Spillers).

effects." To that end, H.R. 40 would do four things: (1) recognize the injustice and inhumanity of slavery; (2) establish the aforementioned commission to study the impact of slavery; (3) study the consequences of racial and economic discrimination on African Americans today; and (4) have the commission recommend to Congress the "appropriate remedies to redress the harm inflicted on living African Americans."[1]

Though most members of the Congressional Black Caucus have cosponsored Conyers's bill, the legislation has not progressed since its first introduction in 1989. In fact, because the bill has never been reported out of committee, members have not had the opportunity to vote on it. That stalling illustrates the deep divisions that reparations proposals produce among Americans and their political leaders. Whether controlled by Democrats or Republicans, the House of Representatives has refused to embrace the issue of reparations as even a possibility. In fact, even though most African American members of Congress support Conyers's bill, a handful refuse to cosponsor it, arguing that the creation of a reparations commission would do more harm than good for modern race relations.[2] In that fissure within the Congressional Black Caucus, and within Congress more generally, lies an excellent example of the major arguments, claims, and limitations that each side on the reparations debate possesses. Though modern issues have naturally informed the debate, these arguments have developed over several decades of reparations activism.

HISTORICAL CONTEXT

One legal scholar has broken down the reparations effort into five major periods: the Civil War era, the early twentieth century, the activism of Marcus Garvey in the 1920s, the modern civil rights movement, and the most recent efforts of the 1990s and early twenty-first century. In each of those periods, reparations activists focused on the social injustice and economic impact of slavery upon generations of African American slaves and their descendants. Opponents rejected those claims in the early periods because of continuing racism and antipathy to revisiting the controversy of slavery; modern opposition is rooted in the belief that establishing restitution for slavery is more harmful than helpful in contemporary race relations. While each side has altered and updated its respective arguments to fit the circumstances of its time, an examination of the historical background of reparations will illustrate the longevity of some pro- and anti-reparations arguments.

The reparations issue actually began on the battlefield. After his stirring March to the Sea, during which thousands of African American slaves in Georgia began trailing his army, General William Tecumseh Sherman issued Special Orders 15. The order called for the immediate confiscation of all lands owned and cultivated by slaveowners from Charleston, South Carolina, to Jacksonville, Florida, and the redistribution of those lands to former slaves. The order granted 40,000 freedpeople "possessory title" to the land, though Sherman stated explicitly that Congress "shall regulate the title." Ignoring the possibility that Congress might regulate the title in favor of the former white landowners, freedpeople in the low country and beyond came to expect their just recompense for being enslaved. Sherman's special order thus created both the promise and the eventual frustration for former slaves and their descendants, for with the end of the war also came the end of Sherman's military power over such matters. Left in the hands of politicians, landowner-ship would be a fleeting and empty promise.[3]

That short-lived taste of landownership and small restitution for being enslaved is as close as African Americans have come to seeing reparations. As a legislative issue, even during the hyper-anti-Confederate sentiment of Radical Reconstruction, reparations received only scant attention as a serious proposal to reorder the South. The first call for slavery reparations in legislative form was made by the highest-profile member of the Radical Republicans, Representative Thaddeus Stevens of Pennsylvania. In 1865, as both the Civil War and slavery were nearing their intertwined ends, Stevens proposed a radical plan for reordering the socioeconomic structure of the seceded states. Based on the wartime policies of General Sherman, Stevens's plan called for the redistribution of all lands owned by former Confederates to former slaves. Using a formula based on the total acreage held by for-mer rebels, and the total number of freedpeople, Stevens's proposal quickly became known as the "40 acres and a mule" plan. Even with the prospect of a more radical Republican Congress—that is, one that championed the civil rights of former slaves—Stevens found the reception for his agenda to be lukewarm. Dead in committee, Stevens's "40 acres and a mule" plan became a powerful rallying cry among freedpeople and remains the most recogniz-able phrase in the reparations debate. It is no coincidence that contemporary leaders of the reparations movement use the failure of the Stevens proposal as the foundation for their legal cases and political arguments.[4]

Little did those freedpeople know that not only would reparations be a pipedream, but also their social and political footing would erode with the onset of Jim Crow segregation during the last quarter of the nineteenth century. During this second period of reparations activism, two African Americans—W.E.B. Du Bois and Callie House—and one southern white Democrat—Walter Vaughan—figured most prominently in the reparations debate. Vaughan, a curious reparations activist given his background as the son of an Alabama slaveowner, used his political connections to advocate for the welfare of former slaves. During the 1880s, Vaughan lobbied Congress for the passage of an ex-slave pension fund, which would have used an age-based formula to give slaves a monthly pension ranging from $4 to $15. Even though Vaughan's plan was introduced in Congress and was occasionally sponsored by influential members, it was never passed; most curiously for today's reparation activists, the main opponents were the lone three black congressmen. Desiring congressional action and federal money for better education and jobs for African Americans, these House members helped to kill the pension idea.[5]

After the stinging defeat, Vaughan joined forces with Callie House, whose barnstorming across the country on behalf of ex-slaves attracted nearly 200,000 members to her National Ex-Slave Mutual Relief Bounty and Pension Association. In 1916, based on taxes collected on cotton production in the late 1860s, House petitioned Congress for $68 million in restitution for the labor of ex-slaves. Opposed on this issue by the major African American organizations such as the NAACP, House found her petition rejected by Congress as well.

One of the many African American leaders opposing Callie House's petition was W.E.B. Du Bois, one of the most important African American political and intellectual figures in U.S. history. In fact, he jeered at efforts of African American farmers seeking $68 million from the U.S. Treasury, arguing that such efforts were as likely to succeed as black men coming to own the moon. Warning African Americans against the dangers of joining "the latest craze," Du Bois nonetheless continued to highlight the high social, economic, and political costs of American society continuing to refuse to deal with the legacy of slavery.[6]

Though Du Bois advocated political moderation on issues such as reparation, he also provided the grounds for seeing reparations as a fitting restitution for the evil of slavery and unfulfilled promises of Reconstruction. In his work *Black Reconstruction in America* (1935), Du Bois argued that Reconstruction's initial promise was grand but that its long-term accomplishments in ameliorating the condition of former slaves was small. He thus concluded that Reconstruction was America's "splendid failure." For the remainder of his career, Du Bois advocated the fulfillment of Reconstruction's lost promise, though he seemed lukewarm at best that reparations were the best means of achieving that goal.[7]

Subsequent efforts in the twentieth century, such as those led by black nationalist Marcus Garvey, culminated in the 1960s with the civil rights movement. The central reparations effort during that period was the lawsuit filed by Robert Brock, an African American attorney and political activist; although the suit stalled in the courts, it kept the reparations issue alive during a time in which African American political efforts were focused on voting rights and desegregation. With those two issues addressed, by the time the civil rights movement begin to wane in 1970s, the issue of reparations again was poised to take center stage among black rights activists. By the mid-1990s, what had been reparations debates between African nations and the Western nations involved in slave trafficking became an internal national debate in the United States.

Brown University

Though congressional proposals and lawsuits form the bulk of reparations activity, one recent case is an excellent example of the deep-running aspects of the reparations debate. In 2003, the president of Brown University, Ruth Simmons, created a committee composed of faculty and students to investigate the university's historic ties to slave traders and to propose how the university would deal with those ties. In establishing Brown's Steering Committee on Slavery and Justice, Simmons hoped to make the university a model for dealing with the legacy of slavery. Herself a descendant of slaves, Simmons said in her announcement that the committee would "help the campus and the nation come to a better understanding of the complicated, controversial questions surrounding the issue of reparations for slavery." Due to issue its report in the spring of 2006, Brown University has become one of the highest-profile reparations cases in the country.[8]

Slavery reparations erupted at Brown, an Ivy League school, in March 2001 after well-known anti-reparations activist David Horowitz paid for an advertisement in the campus newspaper, "Ten Reasons Why Reparations for Blacks Is a Bad Idea—and Racist Too" (discussed later in this chapter). Furious opponents to the ad whipped up a palpable fervor on campus, which in turn engendered more support for the advertisement, which did eventually appear in the paper. At the root of the debate, which often took the form of typical free speech and free press debates, was the involvement of Brown University's early benefactors in slavery and the slave trade.[9]

Though the university's namesake, Nicholas Brown Jr., was an ardent abolitionist in the nineteenth century, his family was one of Rhode Island's most successful group of slave traders. Moreover, the university's founder, Reverend James Manning, accepted large donations from people associated with slavery and the slave trade, though he himself freed the only slave he owned. With several hundred slave-trading voyages, and more than 100,000 enslaved Africans, routed through Providence, the issue of the Brown family's involvement does not involve only a small number of slaves. Creating tremendous wealth, the Browns donated so much of it to the university that it changed its name from Rhode Island College in 1805. John Brown, one of the university's largest donors in the 1790s, made almost all of his wealth from the lucrative slave-trading business that he founded.[10]

Not alone among universities in its early connection to benefactors involved in slavery, Brown University has attempted to be proactive in dealing with its past. Undoubtedly, a combination of factors led to President Simmons's decision to establish the Committee on Slavery and Injustice. In addition to the campuswide tensions provoked by the Horowitz ad, threats by attorneys involved in reparations lawsuits certainly earned the attention of Brown's administrators. In addition to suing corporations that benefited financially from slavery, those attorneys mentioned by name Brown, Yale, and Harvard Law School, all of which received large donations in the eighteenth and nineteenth centuries from benefactors whose wealth grew, at least in part, out of their investment in slavery or the slave trade. Though no legal action has been initiated against those (or other) universities, the Brown administrators strongly desired to avoid that negative publicity. Finally, although President Simmons has been quiet about her private opinion on the outcome of the committee's findings, her family history and her position as the first African American president of an Ivy League school contributed to the decision. Forthright in her unique position, Simmons said, "I don't think there can be a person with a better background for dealing with this issue than me. If I have something to teach our students, if I have something to offer Brown, it's the fact that I'm a descendant of slaves."[11] When the committee does finally release its report, it undoubtedly will face serious scrutiny by reparations supporters and opponents alike and will probably impact the trajectory of the debate in the political arena.

The Brown example has already prompted another institution, the University of Alabama, to confront its past ties to slavery. In April 2004, President Robert Witt said that the university, founded in 1831, was ready to "look back" at its history, which included faculty members owning slaves and slaves serving as workers at the school. After ordering the construction of grave markers where two of the university's slaves are buried, President Witt also asked the Faculty Senate to consider a formal apology.[12] Less than a week later, that body voted 36–1 to issue the apology. With several other southern universities likely involved with slavery, supporters of the apology at the University of Alabama predicted that their institution would be merely the first in a succession of schools to take such action. Though issuing an apology helps to heal race-based social wounds, the upcoming decision by Brown University, pending legal action, and the uncertain future for H.R. 40 may all blunt any positive impact that actions such as the University of Alabama's have on correcting those mistakes of the past.[13]

FRAMING THE ISSUE

Proponents of reparations have developed a thorough argument in favor of their position, which is rooted in four major rationales: moral, economic, political, and social.[14] Filing lawsuits against corporations, angling for the creation of a federal commission to investigate reparations, and pressuring city councils to pass resolutions in favor of such a commission have given supporters a high-profile strategy for galvanizing their side. On the other hand, opponents of reparations reject the proposal on the grounds that reparations would cause more harm than good for modern race relations. They also cite practical concerns—such as the task of deciding how much money is appropriate; who receives the money; and why contemporary Americans, whose ancestors may not have been involved in slavery, should be saddled with the bill—as arguments against reparations. Often framing their opposition as a cultural challenge, opponents have thus far been successful in preventing victory in the courts or in Congress.

SUPPORTERS OF REPARATIONS

The most commonly mentioned rationale for slavery reparations rests on the modern assessment of slavery as a moral evil that stains the country's past. Supporters of reparations point to a handful of well-known cases from other periods when the victimized groups received reparations from a government entity because of evil done to them. For example, reparations proponents often cite Congress's 1988 decision to grant $20,000 to each of the 60,000 remaining survivors of Japanese American internment camps during World War II; shortly thereafter, Canada followed suit, providing $230 million and a public apology to Japanese Canadians. At the state and local level, in 1994 the Florida legislature appropriated $7 million in restitution to survivors of the 1923 wave of race lynchings and riots in the small community of Rosewood. Finally, most prominently, reparations supporters point to the $60 billion that Germany has paid in reparations for the Holocaust. With so many slavery reparations proponents equating the Holocaust and slavery, that example has been a persuasive one for many observers.

Also key to the pro-reparations position is the abortive history of recompense for slavery. Beginning as the brainchild of William Sherman and a few abolitionist Union generals, reparations became the crux of Thaddeus Stevens's anti-Confederate efforts in the late 1860s. But continued racial prejudice, and abject opposition to such government involvement with ex-slaves, prevented Stevens's proposal from gaining any traction in Congress. Today, supporters point to this lost opportunity of providing slaves with "40 acres and a mule" as legal and political grounds for demanding restitution today. Though the price tag has gotten considerably steeper since the 1860s, as is discussed subsequently, supporters argue that it is only appropriate that the federal government pay this old, and significant, debt.

Economic factors also form an important component of the pro-reparations groups. Supporters argue that the inability of slaves to pass on even a modicum of wealth to subsequent generations has snowballed into a massive economic disadvantage for African Americans: lower property ownership, estates of less value, and a higher proportion of their ethnic group working in lower-paying service jobs are all facets of modern African American life that reparations supporters point to as evidence of slavery's long-term impact. Consequently, pro-reparations activists attempt to estimate the value of unpaid wages to their enslaved ancestors, as well as the value of lost interest over 140 years. With those estimates ranging from $1.4 trillion to $10 trillion, the price tag for restitution is steep. But, say supporters, so have been the economic and social consequences for generations of African Americans.

Indeed, reparations supporters draw close parallels between these long-standing economic problems and some long-term social problems within the African American community. The subject of a heated debate in some African American circles—including such organizations as the NAACP and the Rainbow/PUSH Coalition, and prominent individuals such as black entertainer Bill Cosby—these social issues, which range from low literacy rates to low-paying jobs, are the consequences, supporters say, of slavery. In fact, in the 1960s, then-federal policy analyst Daniel Patrick Moynihan concluded that such social problems were indeed the legacy of slavery, and that the federal government ought to use its ability to help correct them. Although lambasted in the 1960s for perpetuating dangerous stereotypes of African Americans, the so-called Moynihan Report today provides intriguing evidence for the types of links between slavery and the modern African American community that reparations supporters use to make their case.[15]

One of the most prominent reparations supporters is Randall Robinson, founder of TransAfrica Forum. In several books, most notably *The Debt What America Owes to Blacks,* Robinson outlines the reasons why providing reparations is a good idea. Seeing financial restitution as just one aspect of the reparations debate, Robinson also argues for a comprehensive solution:

> There is much new fessing-up that white society must be induced to do here for the common good. First, it must own up to slavery and acknowledge its debt to slavery's contemporary victims. It must, at long last, pay that debt in massive restitutions made to America's only involuntary members. It must help to rebuild the black esteem it destroyed.... It must rearrange the furniture of its national myths, monuments, lores, symbols, iconography, legends, and arts to reflect the contributions and sensibilities of all Americans.... It must recast its lying face.[16]

Just five years after penning that rousing support for reparations, Robinson "gave up on America" by moving to St. Kitts in the Caribbean. Calling America a wasted opportunity, and frustrated by the virtual lack of momentum by reparations supporters, Robinson represents the level of frustration on the pro-reparations side of the debate.[17]

The Lawsuits

Supported by activists such as Randall Robinson, several African American civil rights groups—and some African American individuals—have filed a host of lawsuits aimed at securing restitution for slavery. Targeting both the federal government and corporations, these high-profile cases are the vehicles by which pro-reparations supporters believe they have the best chance of seeing any recompense. Given the languishing of Congressman Conyers's reparations commission bill, the plaintiffs may indeed be the best hope in the near future for the supporters of reparations.

The initial strategy for filing suit lay with the federal government, but because state governments, not the federal government, legalized slavery, reparations supporters determined that corporate America was the next-best target for securing reparations. Given that a host of northern companies that most Americans would not associate with slavery did actually benefit financially from slavery, reparations supporters saw, and have attempted to exploit, the opportunity to try those corporations in court. With several Fortune 500 companies among those targeted, the lawsuits against companies have attracted significant national attention, almost to the extent that they serve as the proxy for all the variations of the reparations debate.

In 2003, two African American women in Illinois filed a civil lawsuit against several major American corporations for their roles in slavery. Hannah Hurdle-Toomey and Marcelle Porter, both descendants of slaves, claimed that the companies benefited financially from the genocidal institution of slavery, and that they therefore bear a legal obligation to repair that history. Grouped together with eight similar class-action lawsuits originally filed in New York, New Jersey, Texas, and Louisiana, the suit by Hurdle-Toomey and Porter attracted national attention because of the estimated damages, $1 trillion. The list of defendants also explains the public's interest: FleetBoston Financial Corporation, CSX Corporation, Aetna Insurance, Brothers Harriman, New York Life Insurance, Norfolk Southern Corporation, Lehman Brothers brokerage firm, Lloyd's of London, Union Pacific Railroad, JP Morgan Chase Manhattan Bank, Westpoint Stevens, R. J. Reynolds Tobacco, Brown and Williamson, Liggett Group, Loews, Canadian National Railway, Southern Mutual Insurance, and American International Group. Representing practically every industry in the nation, and facing charges of benefiting financially from either transporting, insuring, or mortgaging slaves, these corporations scrambled to limit both the potential legal and public relations damage.[18]

In an effort to minimize the criticism that reparations constitute only a "money grab" for individual African Americans, Lionel Jean-Baptise, the lawyer for the two Illinois plaintiffs, argued for any damages awarded to go to a trust fund for African American social programs. "It's not about individuals, it's about broad community seeking capital to rebuild our community," Jean-Baptise said in early 2004. "We need a Marshall Plan to help our community. This is a collective remedy." In making the purposeful connection between reparations and the American plan to rebuild post–World War II Europe, Jean-Baptiste is tapping into a fairly clear history of American generosity in righting wrongs and helping the world's needy.[19]

In spite of their arguments, however, the lawsuit was dismissed by U.S. District Judge Charles Norgle in January 2004. Most damaging to the future prospects of such legal efforts, the jurist pinpointed one of the weak spots in the pro-reparations position: "Plaintiffs cannot establish a personal injury by merely identifying tort victims and alleging a genealogical relationship."[20] Though the judge acknowledged "the historic injustices and the immorality of the institution of human chattel slavery in the United States," he concluded in his 75-page opinion that the plaintiffs' claims were "beyond the constitutional authority of this court." He also ruled that the case did not establish a sound legal rationale for the plaintiffs needing restitution so long after the statute of limitations had expired. Ultimately, Norgle observed, reparations would have to be dealt with in the political arena, namely by Congress.[21]

Undeterred by their setback in Chicago district court, reparations advocates seeking legal redress have regrouped. In the immediate aftermath of the defeat, Roger Wareman, lead attorney for the plaintiffs, conducted several national interviews in which he insisted that the legal fight was not done. Though the status of the lawsuit remains uncertain, attorneys plan either to appeal Judge Norgle's decision or to refile the case with him or another judge. In any case, reparations advocates reject the judge's claim that the issue should be decided only in the political arena.[22]

Separate legal efforts have been filed since the Chicago suit's dismissal. Most prominently, R. J. Reynolds became the target of a new suit filed in New Jersey. The difference between it and the new suit is that the new plaintiffs attempt to prove something that was lacking in the Chicago case: that the company actually enslaved, rather than was involved directly with, one of their ancestors.[23] One way the legal team has attempted to establish that link is through DNA evidence, which the reparations attorneys argue shows a clear connection between descendants of slaves and their African ancestors.[24] Though that case has not yet made its way through the courts, Deadria Farmer-Paellman, the lead plaintiff and initiator of the lawsuit, illustrates the determination of the litigants in eventually winning their case: "My grandfather always talked about the 40 acres and a mule we were never given. These companies benefited from working, stealing and breeding our ancestors, and they should not be able to benefit from these horrendous acts."[25] Using an old historical claim to buttress their legal case, Farmer-Paellman and other reparations plaintiffs still see the courts as the best venue for securing restitution.

City Resolutions

Pro-reparations activists have also used another tactic with some success: the lobbying of city councils to support the creation of a national commission for the study of slavery reparations. City councils in Atlanta, Chicago, Cleveland, Detroit, Dallas, Fort Worth, Nashville, Philadelphia, and Washington, D.C.—as well as dozens of smaller cities—have already passed resolutions supporting Representative Conyers's slavery commission bill. Chicago's city council has taken the additional step of becoming the first major city in the country to pass an ordinance requiring that companies doing business with the city disclose any historic ties to slavery. The organization leading such efforts is NDABA, named after an African term that means "the big sitting-down," or meeting. Wanting the nation to have an open, "big" debate over the issue of slavery, NDABA activists have targeted potentially friendly city councils to produce the momentum needed to gather their goal of one million signatures nationwide in support of the slavery commission bill. Thomas Muhammad, one of the organization's leaders in northern Texas, argues that "reparations isn't just about money. It's about what you will learn from yourself." Helping a handful of activists push their agenda before the Dallas City Council, Muhammad concluded, "It is our belief that the reparations movement is the most important movement of our time and is the primary answer for the wholesale healing of black people's ill in America."[26] Concurring with the reparations supporters, the Dallas City Council agreed, becoming the most recent major city to support the Conyers bill.

The strategy of targeting city councils has almost always provoked huge public outcries in the locales in which NDABA and allied organizations have called for pro-reparations resolutions. Most notable has been a raging reparations controversy in Houston, where members of the National Black United Front have appealed to the city council for support. Though rejected by the mayor and city council in August 2002, the NBUF activists tried again in early 2004, thinking that the new mayor and council might be more receptive. Instead, the leading proponent for action by the Houston City Council, Kofi Taharka, was escorted from the city council meeting when he refused to give up the podium designated for citizens' comments. This prompted a citywide tempest in which several pro-reparations council members criticized Mayor Bill White for ordering Taharka's removal, and for refusing to place reparations on the council agenda.[27]

"I understand and sympathize about the need to dialogue," the mayor concluded. "But I don't think there is any consensus about reparations and compensation. This is a highly charged issue, and that makes it more divisive." Smarting at the mayor's assessment that local government serves its constituents better by focusing on improving traffic and the local economy, NBUF members in Houston continue to attend the weekly council meetings until the mayor relents. One such activist, Minister Robert Muhammad, called the mayor's comments "candy-coated cyanide" and concluded that the mayor "gave us nothing of substance."[28] With pro- and anti-reparations people digging in their heels so firmly, it is no surprise that the issue has embroiled even local communities.

State Resolutions

Emboldened by their growing success at convincing city governments to support the Conyers bill, reparations supporters have begun soliciting similar action from state legislatures across the country. Four states—California, Florida, Louisiana, and Maryland—have passed resolutions supporting Representative Conyers's bill in the U.S. House of Representatives, while three other state legislatures—in New Jersey, New York, and Texas—are considering or have considered similar action.[29] In Maryland, the state General Assembly resolution centered on the lack of an official apology by the federal government for slavery. Using the terminology of the 2001 United Nations World Conference Against Racism—that slavery and the transatlantic slave trade were "crimes against humanity"—the Maryland resolution whipped up significant fervor across the state over its hyperbolic language. One critic, writing in the most prominent newspaper in Maryland, remarked that one must "wonder how objective any commission would be."[30]

OPPONENTS OF REPARATIONS

While not denying the moral evil of slavery, opponents of reparations for slavery have developed an equally thorough position as that of the proponents. Focused mainly on two rationales—the problem of saddling modern white Americans with debt that they and their ancestors may not have been responsible for, and the practical problem of distributing the money—opponents enjoy, at least in the early twenty-first century, an advantage in public opinion. According to several public opinion surveys, approximately three-quarters of the American populace oppose reparations for slavery. At least for the time being, the arguments pushed by opponents do represent majority opinion.

Critics of the reparations agenda have serious problems with the moral and practical issue of saddling modern Americans with a debt from the past. Given that in 1860 only 12 percent of white Southerners (2% of whites nationally) owned slaves, reparations opponents argue that the overwhelming majority of whites in modern American society are not descended from slaveowning families. Making those people pay, opponents argue, is nearly as unjust as the institution of slavery itself. Though reparations supporters counter that a host of whites—from overseers, to small farmers who occasionally hired slaves on a temporary basis, to northern merchants whose businesses profited from slavery—all were complicit in perpetuating the evil of slavery, the difficulty of pinpointing all of the people involved in slavery has stunted the growth of the reparations movement.

Indeed, for many Americans who oppose reparations, those logistical problems make reparations a nonstarter. With tens of millions of immigrants and the natural ethnic intermarrying that occurred as a result, opponents argue that it is impossible to penalize any specific group's descendants for the evils of slavery. William Raspberry, a prominent African American newspaper columnist, sees reparations for events such as the 1921 Tulsa race riot and the segregation of public schools after the 1954 Brown decision as easier to handle logistically. Trying to navigate over one hundred years of history, however, seems impossible. "The problem of sorting out damages, victims, and perpetrators," Raspberry concludes, "is just too great."[31] Likewise, Yale Law School professor Peter Schuck, an opponent of reparations, explains, "You have to decide who's black in a society where a large, growing number of people are of mixed blood."[32]

Professor Schuck, who has written extensively on modern diversity issues, argues that the reparations movement is "misguided" because of a host of moral, political, and logistical problems. Most important among these reasons, defining the beneficiaries and the payers presents serious ethical and practical challenges. Schuck asks, "Would beneficiaries have to show that American slavery caused their current condition? What if they would otherwise have been killed or enslaved by their African captors, or sold to non-American masters?" The case for reparations for African Americans is considerably more muddled, Schuck argues, than other examples of reparations, such as those paid to survivors of Japanese American internment camps. Finally, in what has become an increasingly popular refrain among opponents of reparations, Schuck raises the possibility that affirmative action has been an effective reparations tool not only for African Americans but for the handful of historically oppressed groups in American history.[33] In that sense, Schuck and other contemporary opponents mimic the position of earlier critics such as W.E.B. DuBois.

Opponents likewise reject the notion that white society as a whole owes a debt to African Americans, given that poverty strikes all ethnic groups, and given that the civil rights movement of the mid-twentieth century succeeded in correcting most of the longstanding institutional racism in the United

States. In fact, many opponents blame modern factors, not slavery, for the educational deficiencies, social problems, and economic issues that reparations supporters use as evidence for the need for reparations.

David Horowitz

The most prominent opponent to reparations is the cultural critic and political activist David Horowitz. Inserting himself into the debate in 2001, Horowitz, president of the Center for the Study of Popular Culture, bought full-page ads highlighting the major arguments against reparations. Headlined "Ten Reasons Why Reparations for Blacks Is a Bad Idea—and Racist Too," Horowitz's advertisement touched a nerve among supporters and opponents alike. In addition to making the typical claims of reparations opponents, Horowitz also included a handful of new arguments. For example, given that 3,000 African Americans owned slaves in the antebellum South, Horowitz charged that their descendants, if reparations became a reality, ought to be financially responsible as well.[34]

Moreover, Horowitz rejected the notion that "only whites have benefited from slavery." Positing that all Americans benefited from the wealth generated from slavery, Horowitz suggests that it is impossible to delineate one ethnic group from another when it comes to the long-term economic benefits associated with slavery. In fact, as Horowitz mentions often, the gross national product of African Americans would rank them, if they were a nation, as the 10th most prosperous country in the world. With per capita incomes as much as 50 times that of some of their African counterparts, African Americans, Horowitz argues, have in the long term benefited from their ancestors' forced migration to the United States.

The maelstrom surrounding Horowitz's ad illustrates the high tensions that exist over the issue of reparations. That debate raged the hottest on university campuses, where Horowitz's ad was rejected by newspaper editors on some campuses and provoked debates on others. A longtime critic of political correctness, David Horowitz used the censorship of some campus newspaper editors to strengthen his cause; calling the newspaper editors "brownshirts" after the Nazi censorship police galvanized supporters and opponents of reparations alike. One critic of Horowitz suggested that the editors who rejected the advertisement did more to stir up anti-reparations sentiment than if they had simply taken his money, run the ad, and written an editorial disagreeing with it.[35] By targeting college campuses, Horowitz succeeded in making the reparations issue an open debate, as well as illustrating how possible it was that the proposals may someday become a reality. That alone has engendered a tremendous backlash to the pro-reparations position.

Helps or Hurts Race Relations?

Indeed, much of that backlash has centered on reparations doing more harm than good for race relations. Opponents argue that the increased consternation over reparations merely reverses some of the impressive, if not complete, gains against racism achieved since the mid-twentieth century. Even some supporters of affirmative action who oppose reparations are concerned that the reparations agenda, as a sort of proxy debate for affirmative action, damages the long-term prospects for such policies. Opponents, in emphasizing the long passing of time since slavery's demise, look distrustfully upon the aims of reparations supporters.

Given the deep division over the issue, it is unlikely that it will be resolved soon. Moreover, with the number of Latinos surpassing the number of African Americans in a recent update to the 2000 federal census, the nation's changing social and ethnic dynamics may very well complicate the argument of reparations proponents. Nonetheless, with several more cities considering resolutions that would support the creation of a federal reparations commission, and with reparations-based lawsuits still in the legal system, it is also unlikely that Americans of the twentieth-first century have heard the last about reparations for slavery.

QUESTIONS AND ACTIVITIES

1. Organize your class into two groups—one will support reparations, the other will oppose reparations. Debate the issue. What are the most persuasive arguments in favor of reparations? What are the most persuasive arguments against reparations?

2. Discuss the other examples of reparations in American and world history. Compare and contrast them to the slavery reparations proposals.

3. Have the two groups discuss the legacy of slavery. Exactly what is the legacy of slavery in the United States? Is it possible to identify links between modern issues and slavery?

4. To what extent do affirmative action programs address the long-term impact of slavery?

5. To what extent is affirmative action a valid reparations program?

6. Are there other strategies for addressing this issue that both supporters and opponents are missing?

7. Hispanic Americans have recently surpassed African Americans as the largest ethnic minority in the United States. Will this demographic change have any effect on the reparations debate? What is the effect, if any?

8. Will the reparations debate ever be resolved? Why or why not?

NOTES

1. Congressman John Conyers, Jr., Major Issues—Reparations Page, http://www.house.gov/conyers/news_reparations.htm.

2. Lawrie Balfour, "Unreconstructed Democracy: W.E.B. Du Bois and the Case for Reparations," *American Political Science Review* 97 (2003), 33–44.

3. James M. McPherson, *Ordeal by Fire: The Civil War and Reconstruction* (New York: McGraw Hill, 2001), 432.

4. Ibid., 547–49.

5. David W. Blight, "If You Don't Tell It Like It Was, It Can Never Be as It Ought to Be," Keynote Talk at the Conference on Yale, New Haven, and American Slavery, 2003, http://www.yale.edu/glc/events/memory.htm.

6. Balfour, "Unreconstructed Democracy."

7. W.E.B. Du Bois, *Black Reconstruction in America: An Essay toward a History of the Part Which Black Folk Played in the Attempt to Reconstruct Democracy in America, 1860–1880* (Cleveland: Meridan Books, 1964 [1935]), 708.

8. Stephanie Clark, "Students Unclear about Mission of Slavery and Injustice Committee," *Brown Daily Herald*, 20 April 2004.

9. Brooke Donald, "Brown Begins Two-Year Inquiry into Its Connections to Slavery," Associated Press Wire, 21 March 2004.

10. Ibid.

11. Pam Belluck, "Brown University to Examine Possible Reparations for Slavery," *New York Times*, 15 March 2004.

12. Jay Reeves, "University of Alabama Moves to Admit Slavery Ties," Associated Press Wire, 16 April 2004.

13. Martin Caddell, "Faculty Senate Apologizes to Descendants of Slaves," *Crimson White*, 21 April 2004.

14. "The Afrocentric Experience: Reparations," http://www.swagga.com/reparation.htm.

15. Daniel Patrick Moynihan, *The Negro Family: The Case for National Action* (Washington, D.C.: Office of Policy Planning and Research, U.S. Dept. of Labor, 1965).

16. Randall Robinson, *The Debt: What America Owes to Blacks* (New York: Penguin Books, 2000), 107–8.

17. Randall Robinson, *Quitting America: The Departure of a Black Man from His Native Land* (New York: Dutton, 2004).

18. Al Swanson, "Reparations Fight Will Continue," United Press International Wire, 27 January 2004.

19. Carlos Sadovi, "Some of the Bigger Names in Corporate America are Named in a Class-Action Suit," *Calgary Herald* (Alberta, Canada), 18 January 2004.

20. Mary Mitchell, "Court Defeat Isn't the End of the Reparations Movement," *Chicago Sun-Times*, 27 January 2004.

21. Mike Robinson, "Federal Judge Dismisses Slave Reparations Suit," Associated Press Wire, 27 January 2004.

22. Transcript of *Tavis Smiley Show*, National Public Radio, 28 January 2004.

23. Donald W. Patterson, "RJR Named in Suit Seeking Slavery Reparations," *Greensboro News & Record*, 31 March 2004.

24. James Cox, "Descendants of Slaves Accuse Companies of Genocide," *USA Today*, 30 March 2004.

25. Monica Moorehead, "Reparations & Black Liberation," *Workers' World*, 6 June 2002, http://www.millionsforreparations.com/lawsuit-ww.html.

26. James Ragland, "Thinking of Cosby, Reparations Effort," *Dallas Morning News*, 8 June 2004.

27. Kristen Mack, "Police Take Activist Out of Council Meeting," *Houston Chronicle*, 31 March 2004.

28. Kristen Mack, "Mayor Rejects Reparations Demand," *Houston Chronicle*, 14 April 2004.

29. Press Release by Congressman John M. Conyers Jr., 28 March 2003, http://www.house.gov/judiciary_democrats/reparationschicagopr32803.pdf.

30. Gregory Kane, "Whereas, the Legislators Are Misguided...," *Baltimore Sun*, 3 April 2004.

31. William Raspberry, "Reparations Raise Ethical, Financial Questions," *Deseret Morning News* (Salt Lake City), 2 March 2004.

32. Sadovi, "Some of the Bigger Names in Corporate America."

33. Peter H. Schuck, "Slavery Reparations: A Misguided Movement," *Jurist*, 9 December 2002, http://jurist.law.pitt.edu/forum/forumnew78.php.

34. David Horowitz, "Ten Reasons Why Reparations for Blacks Is a Bad Idea for Blacks—and Racist Too," *Front Page Magazine*, 3 January 2001, http://www.frontpagemag.com.

35. Joan Walsh, "Who's Afraid of the Big, Bad Horowitz?" *Salon*, 9 March 2001, http://www.salon.com.

SUGGESTED READING

"The Afrocentric Experience: Reparations," http://www.swagga.com/reparation.htm.

Balfour, Lawrie. "Unreconstructed Democracy: W.E.B. Du Bois and the Case for Reparations." *American Political Science Review* 97 (2003): 33–44.

Belluck, Pam. "Brown University to Examine Possible Reparations for Slavery." *New York Times*, 15 March 2004.

Blight, David W. "If You Don't Tell It Like It Was, It Can Never Be As It Ought to Be." Keynote Talk at the Conference on Yale, New Haven, and American Slavery, 2003, http://www.yale.edu/glc/events/memory.htm.

Browne, Robert S. "The Economic Case for Reparations to Black America." *American Political Science Review* 62 (1972): 39–46.

Caddell, Martin. "Faculty Senate Apologizes to Descendants of Slaves." *Crimson White*, 21 April 2004.

Clark, Stephanie. "Students Unclear about Mission of Slavery & Injustice Committee." *Brown Daily Herald*, 20 April 2004.

Conyers, Congressman John, Jr. Press Release, 28 March 2003, http://www.house.gov/judiciary_democrats/reparationschicagopr32803.pdf.

———. Major Issues—Reparations Page, http://www.house.gov/conyers/news_reparations.htm.

Cox, James. "Descendants of Slaves Accuse Companies of Genocide." *USA Today*, 30 March 2004.

Donald, Brooke. "Brown Begins Two-Year Inquiry into Its Connections to Slavery." *Associated Press Wire*, 21 March 2004.

DuBois, W.E.B. *Black Reconstruction in America: An Essay toward a History of the Part Which Black Folk Played in the Attempt to Reconstruct Democracy in America, 1860–1880.* Cleveland: Meridan Books, 1964 [1935].

Horowitz, David. "Ten Reasons Why Reparations for Blacks Is a Bad Idea for Blacks—and Racist Too." *Front Page Magazine,* 3 January 2001, http://www.frontpagemag.com.Kane, Gregory. "Whereas, the Legislators Are Misguided..." *Baltimore Sun,* 3 April 2004.

Mack, Kristen. "Police Take Activist Out of Council Meeting." *Houston Chronicle,* 31 March 2004.

———. "Mayor Rejects Reparations Demand." *Houston Chronicle,* 14 April 2004.

McPherson, James M. *Ordeal by Fire: The Civil War and Reconstruction.* New York: McGraw Hill, 2001.

Mitchell, Mary. "Court Defeat Isn't the End of the Reparations Movement." *Chicago Sun-Times,* 27 January 2004.

Moorehead, Monica. "Reparations & Black Liberation." *Workers' World,* 6 June 2002, http://www.millionsforreparations.com/lawsuit-ww.html.

Moynihan, Daniel Patrick. *The Negro Family: The Case for National Action.* Washington, D.C.: Office of Policy Planning and Research, U.S. Dept. of Labor, 1965.

National Public Radio, Transcript of *Tavis Smiley Show,* 28 January 2004.

Patterson, Donald W. "RJR Named in Suit Seeking Slavery Reparations." *Greensboro News & Record,* 31 March 2004.

Ragland, James. "Thinking of Cosby, Reparations Effort." *Dallas Morning News,* 8 June 2004.

Raspberry, William. "Reparations Raise Ethical, Financial Questions." *Deseret Morning News* (Salt Lake City), 2 March 2004.

Reeves, Jay. "University of Alabama Moves to Admit Slavery Ties." Associated Press Wire, 16 April 2004.

Robinson, Mike. "Federal Judge Dismisses Slave Reparations Suit." Associated Press Wire, 27 January 2004.

Robinson, Randall. *The Debt: What America Owes to Blacks.* New York: Penguin Books, 2000.

———. *Quitting America: The Departure of a Black Man from his Native Land.* New York: Dutton, 2004.

Schuck, Peter H. "Slavery Reparations: A Misguided Movement." *Jurist,* 9 December 2002, http://jurist.law.pitt.edu/forum/forumnew78.php.

Swanson, Al. "Reparations Fight Will Continue." United Press International Wire, 27 January 2004.

Walsh, Joan. "Who's Afraid of the Big, Bad Horowitz?" *Salon,* 9 March 2001, http://www.salon.com.

Videos

Eisler, John. *Slave Reparations.* Cinema Guild, 2003. 52 min. Described as examining "the current controversy over the issue of slave reparations, addressing the most often voiced objections ('It's long over,' 'I had nothing to do with it,'

'Affirmative Action is enough,' etc.) to the claim for financial restitution to the ancestors of slaves for the wealth created by black labor in previous centuries." See http://www.cinemaguild.com for more information.

Isitan, Isaac. *By Any Means Necessary.* Cinema Guild, 1997. 52 min. Described as exploring the "two leading currents in contemporary African-American thinking—Afrocentrism and the reparations movement—both of which represent the black community's response to centuries of political, economic and social oppression." See http://www.cinemaguild.com for more information.

Web Sites

Congressman John M. Conyers Jr. Official Web Site, http://www.house.gov/conyers/news_reparations.htm.

Millions for Reparations, http://www.millionsforreparations.com.

National Black United Front (NBUF), http://www.nbuf.org.

National Coalition of Blacks for Reparations in America (N'COBRA), http://www.ncobra.org.

We Won't Pay, http://www.wewontpay.com/info.htm. An anti-reparations Web site, the link listed contains a list of pro- and anti-reparations groups.

2

CRIME AND PUNISHMENT

In one of the most famous political advertisements in American history, the presidential campaign of George H. W. Bush in 1988 highlighted the rape of a white woman committed by a furloughed prisoner from Massachusetts. The inmate, an African American man named Willie Horton, had been granted a temporary release from prison by Bush's opponent, Massachusetts governor Michael Dukakis. The devastating ad's purpose was to expose Dukakis's alleged overly liberal policy positions, particularly what the Bush campaign characterized as the governor being "soft" on crime. Even though a version of the hard-hitting commercial had been less effective when used in the Democratic primaries by Senator Al Gore, in the general election campaign it politically debilitated Dukakis. Once leading the race by as many as 17 points, he lost to Vice President Bush by an overwhelming margin.[1]

The commercial was, and remains, controversial not only because of its negative tone, but because of the imagery used. The potency of showing a furloughed African American prisoner was not lost on Bush's critics, who argued that money and energy would be better spent reforming the prison system. As an icon of America's failing prison system—and of the disproportionate share of prison cells occupied by black men—Willie Horton energized supporters and opponents of reform alike.

The image of an imprisoned African American male is one that most Americans have no trouble creating in their minds. The reason is that it takes such little creativeness: African Americans, particularly males, are incarcerated at disproportionately high rates. In what has been portrayed as a crisis for the black community, the overrepresentation of African Americans in U.S. prisons has received considerable attention by public policy analysts, political leaders, and community activists. Even with significantly higher rates of incarceration among all groups in the United States, the historical background of racism and unfair punishment makes this issue particularly charged with emotion. Consequently, many Americans have clamored for wholesale reform in American law enforcement and prison systems, charging that lingering racism results in the high percentage of arrests of African Americans. Opponents of such reforms argue that the statistics simply bear out a tragic social reality—that African Americans are simply more likely to commit crime, and therefore end up in jail. This chapter explores each side in the debate over racism's role in the high rate of incarcerated African Americans.

Three-Strikes Laws

In the early 1990s, one of the dominant political issues was crime. Tired of upward-spiraling crime rates and fearful of the increasing number of drug-related offenses, many Americans demanded dramatic reform to the systems of enforcement, punishment, and imprisonment. One of the most popular reform proposals was mandatory sentencing laws, more commonly known as three-strikes provisions. Using baseball imagery, these policies triggered automatic sentences for felony offenses. After the state of Washington enacted the first three strikes law in 1993, Congress passed a federal version the following

Maximum security inmates at Mississippi State Penitentiary's Unit 17 peer though the security fence in 2002 (AP Wide World Photo/Rogelio Solis, File).

year. By 2004, a total of 26 states had passed such legislation. In some states, such as California, even if the third felony offense is relatively minor—for example, shoplifting—if the offender has two violent or serious felonies on his or her record, the automatic sentence is life in prison.

Long viewed as a magic pill for high crime rates, three strikes laws have been controversial since they were first proposed. One of the central criticisms was, and has been, that these laws discriminate against people of color, namely African Americans and Latinos. With the advantage of 10 years' worth of hindsight, a growing chorus of three-strikes opponents is citing evidence that those criticisms were correct. Most notably, these critics argue, African Americans are 12 times more likely to be sentenced under three-strikes provisions than are whites.[2] Coupled with other examples of possible racism in the criminal justice system, the mandatory sentencing provisions have become the target of many justice reform organizations. In 2002, citing the Eighth Amendment's prohibition against cruel and unusual punishment, the Ninth Circuit Court of Appeals overturned the convictions of two California men jailed through that state's three-strikes law. Though this decision emboldened reform activists, it has not led to sweeping change, as every three-strikes law passed in the 1990s remains in effect.[3]

One reason that the 2002 judicial decision has not resulted in such change is that three-strikes laws have many supporters, and their arguments about those laws helping to reduce crime remain persuasive with many Americans. In California, Bill Jones, the state assemblyman who authored that state's original mandatory sentencing law, credits the provision for reducing crime by nearly half since its approval.[4] Though the actual effects of three-strikes laws are debated, the argument that the laws have been effective in reducing crime is a potent one for supporters of reform to overcome.

HISTORICAL CONTEXT

The history of the American criminal justice and penal systems is replete with reform efforts. Many of those movements were aimed at correcting racial injustice. The earliest reform effort, however, had a more general target: all prisoners. Disturbed by what he considered to be the ineffectual consequences of being imprisoned, British prison reform advocate John Howard traveled the world during the late eighteenth century to promote his idea of proper prisons. In fact, Howard eventually coined the term *penitentiary,* which came from his belief that prisoners should be incarcerated in a way that made them penitent rather than physically and socially scarred. Until the mid-nineteenth century, most American prisons at least roughly followed this model.[5]

After the Civil War, however, the relatively progressive policies toward imprisonment waned as racial tensions pervaded penal policies. The abolition of slavery aggravated the pervasive racism across the country, but particularly in the South, where thousands of ex-slaves migrated in search of better economic and social opportunity. The presence of so many roaming African Americans prompted every former Confederate state to take action against vagabondage. Stiff, excessive punishments for property theft spurred a dramatic increase in the black prison populations of these states.

In addition to a sheer rise in the black incarcerated population, Southern states also created race-based systems of labor for prisoners. Working in what are commonly known as chain gangs, prisoners were forced to conduct grueling labor as part of their punishment. Moreover, the practice of convict leasing, whereby gangs of prisoners were leased by states to contractors, further corrupted the penal system. Under the convict lease system, contractors who obtained temporary title to gangs in turn subcontracted them to a host of business enterprises including railroad companies, timber operations, and levee builders. Most telling about this system of convict leasing was that many gangs were leased to planters, some of whom might actually have owned certain members of the chain gang they were leasing. Combined with other features of postwar African American life, the convict leasing system merely reprised the central features of slavery and incorporated them into the criminal justice system.[6]

In addition, the rise of so-called convict farms, often located on the site of plantations, smacked of the slavery system that had been, at least in official terms, abolished in 1865. Some of the most famous of these institutions, such as Parchman Farm in Mississippi and Angola Farm in Louisiana, became the subject of intense scrutiny by both civil rights and prison reform advocates of the 1870s and 1880s. Interestingly, as the most recent generation of reform supporters clamors for change, they often cite Parchman State Prison and Angola State Prison, both located on the sites of the old convict farms.[7] The 1896 *Plessy v. Ferguson* case, which dictated a policy of "separate but equal" facilities for whites and blacks, merely reinforced the practice of prison farms across the South.

Ironically, the Great Depression ushered in a new wave of reforms, some of which were aimed directly at ending the convict leasing programs. Both the Hawes-Cooper Act (1929) and the Ashurst-Summers Act (1935) effectively illegalized prison labor by allowing states to prohibit the sale of goods manufactured by convict laborers. Though concern for the welfare of prisoners was one impetus for these reforms, the circumstances of economic depression were considerably more important. In particular, two groups—small manufacturers concerned with the low-priced goods created by convict laborers, and increasingly powerful labor unions concerned with those laborers doing work that otherwise would be done by one of their members—fought for the reform. Thus, while a progressive step, these passage of these two pieces of legislation does not necessarily reflect a widespread change in sentiment toward prisoners, whether white, black, or of another ethnic background.[8]

A more deeply seated reform effort took root during the 1960s, which was prompted by the overturning of the *Plessy v. Ferguson* case in the *Brown v. Board of Education* decision (1954). Aimed at both the legal and penal sides of the American criminal justice system, the civil rights movement culminated in many ways with legal reforms that altered the racial bias of Southern courts. A wave of concern for prisoners, too, led many social reformers, both within and separate from civil rights organizations, to push for rehabilitation, counseling, and training for prisoners. As a result, during the 1960s, several states initiated changes to their penal systems that placed less emphasis on punishment and more emphasis on rehabilitation. In 1971, a major revolt at Attica state prison in New York, which was prompted by racial tensions between prisoners and guards, highlighted the need for reforms.[9] For African Americans, these changes seemed to be the long-overdue responses to generations of racial prejudice in criminal justice systems across the country.

McCleskey v. Kemp

In 1987, efforts to reform the criminal justice system's alleged racism culminated in a U.S. Supreme Court decision on the matter. The origins of this case, *McCleskey v. Kemp,* began when Warren McCleskey, an African American man convicted of shooting a police officer during an armed robbery in Georgia, was sentenced to death. McCleskey's attorneys, provided by the NAACP Legal Defense and Education Fund, filed an appeal, seeking to overturn the sentencing based on what he characterized as a subtle but powerful racism in the American criminal justice system. In particular, the lawyer argued, the fact that McCleskey was convicted of murdering a white man dramatically increased his chances of being sentenced to death.[10] McCleskey's attorney based the appeal on an influential statistical study by scholars David Baldus, Charles Pulaski, and George Woodworth. This study concluded that race was often a factor in the sentencing phase of capital murder cases. For example, in cases in which the victim was white, 22 percent of black defendants received a death sentence, whereas only 8 percent of white defendants were sentenced to death. While the authors stopped short of alleging systemic racism in Georgia's criminal justice system, one of the study's other findings seemed to indicate such institutionalized bias: in cases with a white victim, prosecutors sought the death penalty 70 percent of the time when the defendant was black, and only 32 percent of the time when the defendant was white. Though the 11th Circuit Court of Appeals was not swayed by this argument, the McCleskey legal team succeeded in getting the U.S. Supreme Court to hear the case.[11]

In a 5-to-4 decision, the Court rejected McCleskey's arguments, ruling that the evidence presented did not demonstrate a systematic, institutionalized racism. Writing for the majority, Justice Lewis Powell feared using inconclusive evidence to throw "into serious question the principles that underlie our entire criminal justice system." After explaining with thoroughness the finding of the Baldus study, Powell concluded:

> To evaluate McCleskey's challenge, we must examine exactly what the Baldus study may show. Even Professor Baldus does not contend that his statistics prove that race enters into any capital sentencing decisions or that race was a factor in McCleskey's particular case.... At most, the Baldus study indicates a discrepancy that appears to correlate with race. Apparent disparities in sentencing are an inevitable part of our criminal justice system. In light of the safeguards designed to minimize racial bias in the process, the fundamental value of jury trial in our criminal justice system, and the benefits that discretion provides to criminal defendants, we hold that the Baldus study does not demonstrate a constitutionally significant risk of racial bias affecting the Georgia capital sentencing process.[12]

Rejecting further the arguments of McCleskey that his Eighth and Fourteenth Amendment rights had been violated, the five justices of the majority declined to overturn the lower court's ruling.

But the decision was not without dissent. Justice William Brennan wrote that the majority's opinion "seems to suggest a fear of too much justice." In a poignant analysis, Brennan wrote:

> At some point in this case, Warren McCleskey doubtless asked his lawyer whether a jury was likely to sentence him to die. A candid reply to this question would have been disturbing. First, counsel would have to tell McCleskey that few of the details of the crime or of McCleskey's past criminal conduct were more important than the fact that his victim was white.... Finally, the assessment would not be complete without the information that cases involving black defendants and white victims are more likely to result in a death sentence than cases featuring any other racial combination of defendant and victim. The story could be told in a variety of ways, but McCleskey could not fail to grasp its essential narrative line: there was a significant chance that race would play a prominent role in determining if he lived or died.[13]

Not surprisingly, both supporters and opponents of criminal justice reform seized the case as a milestone in their respective efforts. McCleskey supporters, though disappointed by the ruling, recognized that the case might serve as an effective public relations vehicle for future efforts. In the aftermath of the decision, the NAACP legal team vowed to file additional appeals to prevent Warren McCleskey's execution.[14] But those appeals proved futile, as McCleskey was executed in September 1991.[15]

Opponents, on the other hand, have trumpeted the landmark case as an affirmation of the criminal justice system's fairness. In subsequent debates over the death penalty—all of which involve, to some extent, the issue of racial bias—those people opposed to change used the case to illustrate that when before the highest court in the land, the statistics and arguments used by proponents of reform do not hold up to scrutiny. In that sense, then, nearing its 20th anniversary, *McCleskey v. Kemp* remains not only the highest-profile court case in the issue of criminal justice reform, but also an excellent example of the arguments that each side uses.

FRAMING THE ISSUE

As part of the ongoing national debate over racism's continued existence, the controversy over criminal justice reform involves individual activists, prominent political leaders, advocacy organizations, and public policy think tanks. Though activists on each side of the issue have a different interpretation of the problem, they all start with some basic facts. As table 2.1 illustrates, African Americans constitute a share of the U.S. prison population that is disproportionate to their share of the nation's population. In 2003, of the nearly 2.1 million inmates in federal, state, and local prisons, almost 900,000 were African Americans. This 43 percent share of the nation's prison population is 3.5 times African Americans' share of the nation's total population (12 percent). Perhaps even starker is that 12 percent of black men aged 20–29 are imprisoned, compared to 3.7 percent of Hispanic men and 1.6 percent of white men the same age.[16] (As table 2.1 shows, women constitute a disproportionately small share—only 17 percent—of the nation's prison population, which causes activists on this issue to focus on men.)

Though each side starts with these basic figures, the agreement ends there. As a result, the level of rhetoric by both sides has produced a flurry of studies, public debates, and legislative hearings. In the midst of all the various interests at stake, however, it is possible to reduce this complex issue into the most salient points raised by each side. Supporters of criminal justice reform work under the assumption, which seems to be supported by their copious statistical studies, that racism pervades American criminal justice institutions. They use three primary arguments to advance their case: (1) that incarceration rates demonstrate an overwhelming overrepresentation of African

Table 2.1 Number of Inmates in Federal, State, and Local Prisons, by Gender, Race, and Ethnicity, as of June 30, 2003

	Total	White	Black	Hispanic
MEN	1,902,300	665,100	832,400	363,900
WOMEN	176,300	76,100	66,800	28,300

Source: Paige M. Harrison and Jennifer C. Karberg, "Prison and Jail Inmates at Midyear 2003," Bureau of Justice Statistics Bulletin, U.S. Department of Justice

Americans and Latinos; (2) that the practice of racial profiling both illustrates the systematic racism and helps to produce overrepresentation of minorities in prisons; and (3) the massively expanded war on drugs, funded by both the federal government and states, unfairly targets African Americans. As a result, supporters argue, money spent on building new prisons should be diverted to rehabilitation programs and other educational opportunities, both of which, they say, are more effective at reducing crime than stiffer penalties and imprisonment.

On the other hand, opponents of such reforms argue that enough of those alternative methods of treatment already exist, leaving states and the federal government little choice but to seek stiffer penalties and imprisonment as methods of deterrence. That belief in imprisonment as a last alternative represents the opposing position very well. Although some critics of reform proposals do challenge the statistics often cited by activists, the more central claim of opponents is what those statistics really mean. They argue that racism does not produce the overrepresentation of African Americans in prison; instead, they claim, the fact that African Americans commit more crimes produces that disparity. Reform opponents urge that reformers tackle other issues, such as out-of-wedlock births, which some studies have indicated correlate quite directly to the high rate of incarceration among African Americans. Clearly, then, little common ground exists between the two sides. Turning to each position in more detail, as well as examining the arguments of major figures in this debate, will illuminate the many contours of the criminal justice reform controversy in the United States.

SUPPORTERS OF CRIMINAL JUSTICE REFORM

Proponents of reforming the nation's criminal justice system begin with the argument that racism pervades the entire system. They argue that in every step of the criminal justice process—from arrests to convictions to sentencing to imprisonment—African Americans are at the wrong end of racial discrimination. While reform activists recognize that some progress has been made in the realm of civil rights, they often portray the criminal justice system as a lagging arena for the eradication of racism.

Statistics necessarily serve as the argumentative foundation for the reformers' claims. Though such numbers can be both misleading and difficult to follow, a brief capitulation of the most commonly cited ones is necessary to understand the position of supporters. These numbers often illustrate the long-term problem in the criminal justice system. According to U.S. Justice Department statistics, African Americans are imprisoned at seven times the rate of whites, even though they make up a little more than one-tenth the nation's population. A recent Bureau of Justice Statistics study shows that African American children born in the early twenty-first century have considerably higher chances than other ethnic groups of spending time in prison. In 2001, black men faced a 32.2 percent chance of being imprisoned, while Latino men (17.2% chance) trailed, and white men (5.6% chance) faced sharply lower chances. Among women, African American females had a 5.6 percent chance.[17]

As one of the leading advocacy groups for ending racial bias in the criminal justice system, the Justice Policy Institute used such statistical summaries to prompt a wave of reform efforts in the Maryland state legislature. Compiled in a report, "Race and Incarceration in Maryland," the statistics illustrated that in addition to national trends holding true in Maryland, some facets of that state's justice system were even more racially skewed. The study found that black men in Maryland were eight times more likely to be imprisoned than white men, and that black women were 4.2 times more likely to be imprisoned than white women. Moreover, while constituting 28 percent of the state's population, 9 of every 10 inmates convicted of a drug offense are black. In tandem with the finding that three quarters of new prisoners since 1980 have been African Americans, these statistical studies led Maryland's governor and legislature to create new reforms, namely, the use of rehabilitation.[18]

Reform advocates use other statistics to focus on the application of the death penalty, which, as the McCleskey case illustrates, has whipped up considerable emotion on both sides of the reform debate. For example, 4,220 inmates were executed in the United States from 1930 to 1996; of this number, just over half (53%) were black, when during this period African Americans comprised 12 percent of the nation's population. Moreover, as the Baldus study illustrated, prosecutors in Georgia, and presumably in other places, sought the death penalty much more frequently for black defendants than for white defendants.[19]

As in most civil rights–oriented debates, not all supporters of criminal justice reform are African Americans. Many white observers and researchers have taken a leading role in pushing for justice. Perhaps most prominent among this group of reformers is former U.S. president Jimmy Carter. Since leaving office, Carter has been a vocal proponent of prison reform. Using his first-hand experience with racially assigned justice during his tenure as governor of Georgia, Carter has written, "Deliberately or not, punishments are focused on black offenders." Citing statistics showing African Americans are far more likely than whites to be sentenced for crack cocaine violations, Carter has urged state governors and Congress to address what he sees as racial disparities in conviction and sentencing.[20]

Carter's emphasis on drug-related crimes demonstrates one of the reform supporters' most common arguments: that the drug war, which they claim is probably not worth fighting, discriminates grossly against African Americans. Statistics seem to bear out this claim, as 90 percent of inmates who were convicted of drug-related offenses are African American. Marc Mauer, writing in the popular book *The Race to Incarcerate,* published under the auspices of the Sentencing Project, has concluded, "Since 1980, no policy has contributed more to the incarceration of African Americans than the 'war on drugs' ... The drug war has exacerbated racial disparities in incarceration while failing to have any sustained impact on the drug problem."[21]

But what causes this disparity within the war on drugs? Most critics of the drug war as a racially discriminatory effort point out that unlike burglary and similar crimes, which require that police react to a crime based on a citizens' report, waging the drug war effectively means that police must target neighborhoods where drug possession and selling is most prevalent. Though whites, given their numerical superiority in the population, make up the majority of drug users, African Americans have been the chief targets by police. This is likely a result of the nation's largest cities still having racially segregated neighborhoods. Given resources by the federal and state governments to reduce drug crime, local police forces, according to reformers, have concentrated on predominantly black working-class and middle-class neighborhoods. Jason Ziedenberg, an analyst for the Justice Policy Institute, argues, "The police tactics tend to be more focused on neighborhoods where you are more likely to arrest an African American man for a low-level drug offense than if we were to concentrate those resources in a suburb." Though whites and blacks use drugs at roughly the same rate, Ziedenberg says, "We enforce the drug laws more in urban communities, and then we arrest people, and then we convict people, and then they end up in prison."[22] The result, not surprisingly, is that such a high proportion of black Americans end up in prison.

Reform advocates charge that one factor in black overrepresentation in U.S. prisons is the institutionalized racism of local police forces. Supporters of reform typically cite three distinct issues that pertain to municipal law enforcement agencies: hiring practices; the use of force; and, most prominently, racial profiling. High-profile cases such as the beating of Rodney King, an African American man, by Los Angeles police officers in 1991 spurred public debate over systemic racism in local police forces. Recently, although local law enforcement agencies have received generally better marks for increasing ethnic diversity in their departments, concerns over brutality and racial profiling continue. Leading the charge against alleged racism among local police departments, NAACP president Kweisi Mfume stated, "[t]he fact of the matter is, if you are a person of color living in the United States, the police often look at you differently and with a level of suspicion. They always have, and until something is done to raise the level of accountability, they will continue to do so."[23]

Supporters of reform also charge that racism in the justice system produces long-term problems ranging from poverty to lack of education. For example, a Justice Policy Institute report indicated "that 1 out of 10 White male dropouts and half of all African American male dropouts had prison records by their early thirties, and that nearly twice as many African American men in their early 30s have prison records (22%) as Bachelors degrees (12%)."[24] This, in turn, creates a cycle of undereducated and imprisoned African Americans, according to reform advocates. For example, one study in Virginia revealed that less than half of all imprisoned black children even learn sixth-grade skills in reading, writing, and math. With a strong correlation between lack of education and incarceration, critics of the criminal justice system argue that the situation for African Americans is getting worse before it is getting better.

Recently, concerns with the justice system have focused on a politically persuasive argument: spend less on building prisons and more on building schools. Bare numbers have resonated with observers across the country. In Virginia, the state spends approximately $70,000 per year to incarcerate each inmate in a juvenile facility, but only $3,400 to educate that same child. These disparities in spending between prisons and schools have led two prison-reform advocates to observe, "California's budget for its corrections system has risen dramatically over the past 10 years, while recidivism rates have worsened.... With a significant fraction of that cost, we could educate and employ many of those same people. The question must be faced: Are we really leaving no children behind, or are we simply putting them out of sight and, sadly, out of mind?"[25]

OPPONENTS OF REFORM

Critics of criminal justice reform do not ignore that the system once was rife with racism, but they generally reject that racism remains a problem in modern society. To that end, opponents of reform base their arguments on two main positions: (1) the statistics that reform supporters cite are flawed, thereby rendering the racism argument itself flawed; and (2) other social problems, mainly those within the African American community, are to blame for the high rates of arrest, conviction, and incarceration. Based on these two simple, yet politically potent, critiques of the reform position, opponents of criminal justice reform have thus far succeeded in blunting significant, whole-sale changes to the American justice system.

Linda Chavez and the Center for Equal Opportunity

The first argument of reform opponents is that the statistical studies that reform advocates use are flawed and in fact may illustrate the exact opposite of what reformers are trying to demonstrate. The most promi-nent advocate of this position is Linda Chavez, president of the Center for Equal Opportunity (CEO). Both Chavez and CEO promote "colorblind equal opportunity and racial harmony," which means that they typically oppose reform proposals of activists concerned about racism. On the issue of racism in the criminal justice system, CEO conducted a study in the late 1990s that showed that blacks were more likely than whites to avoid conviction.

The CEO study, conducted by Linda Chavez and Robert Lerner, exam-ined convictions in 14 different types of felonies in the 75 largest counties in the country. The study concluded that in all but two of the 14 kinds of felonies—traffic offenses and a catchall category of "other"—whites had higher conviction rates than blacks. Though the conviction rates for each group in many categories were close, in some the disparity was rather large. For example, in cases involving child abuse, extortion, and manslaughter, African American defendants escaped conviction 48 percent of the time, compared to 28 percent of white defendants. In rape cases, the disparity was even starker: African American defendants actually eluded conviction in more than half the cases (51 percent), compared to 25 percent of white defendants. Though only 3 percent of the cases in the study went before a jury—most were decided during the plea-bargaining phase—the statistics remain virtually the same, with African Americans experiencing higher non-conviction rates in cases involving murder, burglary, felony theft, and drug trafficking. Among rape cases that were decided by juries, 83 percent of black defendants, versus 24 percent of white defendants, were acquitted.[26] Obviously, the CEO study, at the very least, provides a compelling counter-argument to the position of reform advocates.

Chavez and Lerner conclude their study by pointing out that "the system has built-in safeguards that prevent racism from running its full course." But they also hint at the possibility of some juries, mainly in predominantly African American cities, practicing Paul Butler's proposal of race-based nullification. In places such as Washington, D.C., and the Bronx, felony acquittal rates for black defendants were much higher than the national average. D.C. Superior Court Judge Reggie B. Walton observed, "I have seen race become more of an issue, and it has resulted in more acquittals and hung juries." Thus, whether through the system working as it should, or through a policy of nullification by black juries for black defendants, the CEO study suggests an alternative view to the criminal justice statistics so often cited by reformers.[27]

Other opponents to reform avoid the statistical arguments. Instead, they argue that factors other than racism—such high poverty rates, lack of education, and out-of-wedlock births—explain the overrepresentation of African Americans in prisons. One Washington, D.C.-based policy organization, the Heritage Foundation, sponsored a study that examined those issues. In the study, the researcher, Patrick Fagan, concluded that in addressing the issue of an apparent racial disparity in arrests and incarceration, "The real variable is not race but family structure." Fagan's empirical evidence illustrated that since the 1960s, the increase in violent crime rates has "paralleled" the rise "in families abandoned by fathers." Intending to complicate the argument that racism by local police forces is to blame for high rates of arrest and incarceration of African Americans, Fagan contends that "high-crime neighborhoods are characterized by high concentrations of families abandoned by fathers." With such a correlation applicable to all ethnic groups, Fagan argues that a more effective public policy decision would be to focus less on the alleged racism in the criminal justice system, and more on the "breakdown of the family" as the underlying cause of African American overrepresentation.[28]

Such an argument is echoed by the prominent black conservative organization Project 21. Mychal S. Massie, a member of Project 21, charges that African Americans themselves, not racist white police officers, are to blame for high incarceration rates. He promotes personal responsibility, claiming that crime "does not have to do with being poor, being black or it being a residual effect of slavery. It has everything to do with not being responsible in one's behavior and our being a country and a system of laws, and we must abide by those."[29] Directly challenging the thinking about racism pervading the criminal justice system, Massie argues, "White guilt and taxpayer dollars are not the cure for those who accuse but fail to take personal responsibility. Self-inflicted victimization should not be a way of life, it should be a crime relentlessly confronted."[30]

As this chorus of people who deny racism's presence in the criminal justice system grows, so does the level of debate. As with most issues in which statistical evidence is employed to advance an argument, the controversy over African American overrepresentation in U.S. prisons produces differing interpretations of what those numbers mean. For the observer, student, and teacher, the best method for cutting through those statistics is to research and recognize the assumptions that each side makes, and that each side wants to "prove" with those statistics. So doing produces an educated debate on a serious public policy matter. With this issue increasing rather than decreasing in rhetoric and significance, it is likely to remain at the forefront of social and political issues facing African Americans in the twenty-first century.

QUESTIONS AND ACTIVITIES

1. Organize your class into two groups—one will support reform of the criminal justice system, the other will oppose reform. Debate the issue. What are the most relevant statistics and arguments of each side? Did your debate change anyone's opinion on the issue?

2. What were the major events, processes, and ideas in the history of racism in the U.S. criminal justice system? Evaluate the most significant turning points in that history.

3. Who are the major figures and what are the major organizations on each side of the debate?

4. Debate the issue of racial profiling. Should it be used by American law enforcement agencies? Have there been any cases in your local area that involve racial profiling?

5. What have been the consequences of the war on drugs? Debate whether it should continue.

6. Explain the controversy over allowing current and former felons the right to vote. What do you think is the appropriate solution?

7. Given what you have read, how do you think this issue will be resolved in the future?

NOTES

1. Samuel Walker, Cassia Spohn, and Miriam DeLone, *The Color of Justice: Race, Ethnicity, and Crime in America* (Belmont, Calif.: Wadsworth, 1996), 49.

2. Vincent Schiraldi and Geri Silva, "Three Strikes; Law That Fails on All Counts," *Los Angeles Times,* 7 March 2004.

3. Earl Ofari Hutchinson, "Three Strikes Law Weakened, but Not Overturned," AlterNet, 14 February 2002, http://www.alternet.org/columnists/story/12418/.

4. Bobby Caina Calvin, "California Initiative Seeks to Rewrite Three-Strikes Law," *Boston Globe,* 12 July 2004.

5. Harry C. Buffardi, "Beginning of the Penitentiary Movement," Corrections History Web site, 1998, http://www.correctionhistory.org/html/chronicl/sheriff/ch6.htm.

6. The History of Jim Crow, http://www.jimcrowhistory.org/history/creating2.htm.

7. David M. Oshinsky, "*Worse Than Slavery*": *Parchman Farm and the Ordeal of Jim Crow Justice* (New York: Free Press, 1997).

8. "Privatizing the Prison System," National Center for Policy Analysis, http://www.ncpa.org/~ncpa/studies/s181/s181n.html.

9. Michael Hill, "A Growing Need for Reform," *Baltimore Sun,* 20 June 2004.

10. Marc Mauer, *The Race to Incarcerate* (New York: New Press, 1999), 130–31.

11. David C. Baldus, Charles Pulaski, and George Woodworth, "Comparative Review of Death Sentences: An Empirical Study of the Georgia Experience," *Journal of Criminal Law and Criminology* 74 (1983): 661–753.

12. *McCleskey v. Kemp,* 481 U.S. 279 (1987). The majority and dissenting opinions can be found at http://www.law.umkc.edu/faculty/projects/ftrials/conlaw/mccleskey.html.

13. Ibid.

14. Laura Mansnerus, "Racial Challenge Rejected; Court Stands Behind the Death Penalty," *New York Times,* 26 April 1987.

15. Dick Williams, "McCleskey's Execution Just End to Long Charade," *Atlanta Journal-Constitution,* 28 September 1991.

16. Paige M. Harrison and Jennifer C. Karberg, "Prison and Jail Inmates at Midyear 2003," Bureau of Justice Statistics Bulletin, U.S. Department of Justice, May 2004 (revised 14 July 2004), http://www.ojp.usdoj.gov/bjs/pub/pdf/pjim03.pdf.

17. Robert B. Bluey, "Experts Differ on Reasons for Widespread Incarceration of Blacks," *Townhall Magazine,* 19 August 2003, http://www.townhall.com/news/politics/200308/CUL20030819a.shtml.

18. Vincent Schiraldi and Jason Ziedenberg, "Race and Incarceration in Maryland," Washington, D.C.: Justice Policy Institute, 2003, http://www.justicepolicy.org/article.php?id = 342#sdfootnote1anc; David Nitkin, "Ehrlich Set to Sign Bill to Expand Prisoner Drug Treatment," *Baltimore Sun,* 11 May 2004.

19. Scott Shepard, "More Blacks Support Death Penalty; Increased Crime May Be Part of Reason," *Atlanta Journal-Constitution,* 18 April 1998.

20. Jill Karson, ed., *Criminal Justice: Opposing Viewpoints* (San Diego: Greenhaven Press, 1998), 20.

21. Mauer, *Race to Incarcerate,* 143.

22. Bluey, "Experts Differ."

23. NAACP Criminal Justice Program, http://www.naacp.org/work/legal/criminaljustice.shtml.

24. Schiraldi and Ziedenberg, "Race and Incarceration in Maryland."

25. Andrew Block and Virginia Weisz, "Choosing Prisoners over Pupils," *Washington Post*, 6 July 2004.

26. Karson, *Criminal Justice: Opposing Viewpoints*, 21–24.

27. Ibid., 24.

28. Patrick F. Fagan, "The Real Root Causes of Violent Crime: The Breakdown of Marriage, Family, and Community," Heritage Foundation Policy Paper, http://www.heritage.org/Research/Crime/BG1026.cfm.

29. Bluey, "Experts Differ."

30. Mychal S. Massie, "Self-Inflicted Victimization," WorldNetDaily, 20 May 2003, http://www.worldnetdaily.com/news/article.asp?ARTICLE_ID=32658.

SUGGESTED READING

Baldus, David C., Charles Pulaski, and George Woodworth. "Comparative Review of Death Sentences: An Empirical Study of the Georgia Experience." *Journal of Criminal Law and Criminology* 74 (1983): 661–753.

Block, Andrew, and Virginia Weisz. "Choosing Prisoners over Pupils." *Washington Post*, 6 July 2004.

Bluey, Robert B. "Experts Differ on Reasons for Widespread Incarceration of Blacks." *Townhall Magazine*, 19 August 2003, http://www.townhall.com/news/politics/200308/CUL20030819a.shtml.

Calvin, Bobby Caina. "California Initiative Seeks to Rewrite Three-Strikes Law." *Boston Globe*, 12 July 2004.

Karson, Jill, ed. *Criminal Justice: Opposing Viewpoints*. San Diego: Greenhaven Press, 1998.

Fagan, Patrick F. "The Real Root Causes of Violent Crime: The Breakdown of Marriage, Family, and Community." Heritage Foundation Policy Paper, http://www.heritage.org/Research/Crime/BG1026.cfm.

Harrison, Paige M., and Jennifer C. Karberg. "Prison and Jail Inmates at Midyear 2003." Bureau of Justice Statistics Bulletin, U.S. Department of Justice, May 2004 (revised 14 July 2004).

Hutchinson, Earl Ofari. "Three Strikes Law Weakened, but Not Overturned." *AlterNet*, 14 February 2002. http://www.alternet.org/columnists/story/12418/.

Mansnerus, Laura. "Racial Challenge Rejected; Court Stands Behind the Death Penalty." *New York Times*, 26 April 1987.

Massie, Mychal S. "Self-Inflicted Victimization." *WorldNetDaily*, 20 May 2003, http://www.worldnetdaily.com/news/article.asp?ARTICLE_ID = 32658.

Mauer, Marc. *The Race to Incarcerate*. New York: New Press, 1999.

McCleskey v. Kemp, 481 U.S. 279 (1987). The majority and dissenting opinions can be found at http://www.law.umkc.edu/faculty/projects/ftrials/conlaw/mccleskey.html.

Nitkin, David. "Ehrlich Set to Sign Bill to Expand Prisoner Drug Treatment." *Baltimore Sun*, 11 May 2004.

Oshinsky, David M. *"Worse Than Slavery": Parchman Farm and the Ordeal of Jim Crow Justice*. New York: Free Press, 1997.

Schiraldi, Vincent, and Geri Silva. "Three Strikes; Law That Fails on All Counts." *Los Angeles Times,* 7 March 2004.

Schiraldi, Vincent, and Jason Ziedenberg. "Race and Incarceration in Maryland." Washington, D.C.: Justice Policy Institute, 2003, http://www.justicepolicy. org/article.php?id = 342#sdfootnote1anc.

Tonry, Michael. *Thinking about Crime: Sense and Sensibility in American Penal Culture.* Oxford. England: Oxford University Press, 2004.

Walker, Samuel, Cassia Spohn, and Miriam DeLone. *The Color of Justice: Race, Ethnicity, and Crime in America.* Belmont, Calif.: Wadsworth, 1996.

Williams, Dick. "McCleskey's Execution Just End to Long Charade." *Atlanta Journal-Constitution,* 28 September 1991.

Videos

The Farm: Life Inside Angola Prison. A&E Entertainment, 1998, http://www. aande.com.

Lichtenstein, Brad. *Ghosts of Attica.* First Run/Icarus Films, 2001. 90 min. http:// www.frif.com.

Web Sites

Center for Equal Opportunity, http://www.ceousa.org.

The History of Jim Crow, http://www.jimcrowhistory.org.

Justice Policy Institute, http://www.justicepolicy.org.

NAACP Criminal Justice Project, http://www.naacp.org/work/legal/criminal justice.shtml.

Project 21 Leadership Network, http://www.project21.org.

3

CULTURAL ASSIMILATION

In December 1996, the School Board of Oakland, California, sparked one of the fiercest cultural debates of the 1990s. Voting unanimously to recognize Ebonics, or black English, as the primary language of African American students, the Oakland School Board touched a nerve that shocked opponents of the decision, as well as galvanized supporters. The maelstrom soon spread to the entire nation, which for the next several years debated the issue in editorial pages, at academic conferences, at town meetings, and on news programs. With several linguists and African American political leaders urging more government entities to recognize Ebonics, the issue has not faded from public view. Instead, in maintaining its position as one of the most important cultural debates dealing with African Americans, the Ebonics controversy has become an illustration of the broader issue of cultural assimilation by black Americans.

Cultural assimilation, which is the idea that one specific culture consciously meshes with the larger national culture, involves more than just Ebonics. Recent controversies involving Kwanzaa, the African American holiday, and usage of the term *African American* also speak to this larger issue of black Americans assimilating with the broader culture of the United States. Even some prominent African Americans, such as entertainer Bill Cosby, have spoken vociferously in favor of the black community doing a better job of consciously molding its own cultural traditions with popular culture. Cosby reflects the arguments of people who propose that blacks assimilate. These arguments rest on the notion that while African American culture ought to maintain its traditions, the continued cultural separation between blacks and

the rest of the country only exacerbates racial problems and, most importantly, keeps African American society from developing fully. Opponents of
assimilation argue that the only way to preserve African American culture is
to keep it separate, enabling it to serve as a source of pride—something that
has been and continues to be lacking among African Americans. This chapter
delves into this debate, looking at the broader issue of assimilation as well as
the specific controversies over Ebonics and Kwanzaa.

Kwanzaa

Today, Kwanzaa, which is Swahili for "first fruit," is widely recognized as
an African American holiday. But some common misconceptions are often
accepted as fact. One of them is that Kwanzaa is the "black Christmas,"
which undoubtedly has gained currency because Kwanzaa begins the day after
Christmas and lasts for seven days. The other most common misunderstand-
ing is that Kwanzaa is an old, long-celebrated African holiday. Propagated
by some early proponents of Kwanzaa to give the holiday more historical
weight, this misconception conceals the relatively recent origins of Kwanzaa
during the American civil rights movement of the 1960s.

Kwanzaa celebration at the Museum of Natural History, December 26, 2004
(AP Wide World Photo/Jennifer Szymaszek).

In 1966, African American activist and scholar Maulana Karenga founded Kwanzaa. Inspired by the 1966 Watts race riots in Los Angeles, Karenga sought a celebration that would move African Americans away from the violence of the 1960s and toward a deeper understanding of their cultural roots. Kwanzaa is appealing to some African Americans because it provides them and their culture with an identity. One organization that promotes the celebration explains that for African Americans, the "pursuit of black culture is the nucleus of Kwanzaa and takes us back to our roots which are in Africa. The spiritual aspects of Kwanzaa are an effort to get away from the over commercialization of the Christian holiday Christmas and Santa Claus. Blacks are searching for identity and Kwanzaa is the natural choice."[1]

Karenga points to the elements of Kwanzaa based on both African and Western ideas as one of the reasons that more blacks have begun to celebrate the holiday. Modeled largely on several "first fruit" celebrations in Africa, Kwanzaa, according to Karenga, allows African Americans "to rescue and reconstruct our history and culture and shape them in our image."[2] Based on seven principles—unity, self-determination, collective work and responsibility, cooperative economics, purpose, creativity, and faith—Kwanzaa has attracted many new celebrants during the last 20 years.[3] From its modest following in December 1966—essentially just Karenga's own family and friends—Kwanzaa has become a popularly celebrated holiday among blacks in the United States, Canada, the Caribbean, and Europe.

Critics, though, charge that Kwanzaa serves to separate African Americans from the national culture of the United States. In particular, they argue that Kwanzaa, in its emphasis on African roots, downplays too much the holidays and celebrations in America that have been influenced by black Americans; in essence, these critics argue, delineating holidays according to ethnic background does more to maintain divisions than it does to heal them. That Kwanzaa is not a so-called authentic African holiday, and that it was borne out of the black nationalist movement that had expressed hostility toward Christians, women, and racial integration, merely underscores the skepticism that critics have regarding the intended effect of the celebration.

Skeptics also argue that the problems in American society that Kwanzaa was founded to critique—namely, the over-commercialization of Christmas—have become problems plaguing Kwanzaa. A recent study claimed that Kwanzaa is a $700 million industry, with greeting cards, gifts, and decorations having significant presence in American retail establishments. While Kwanzaa supporters argue that this is merely a sign that Kwanzaa has become a viable alternative to the European holidays of Christmas and Hanukkah, critics conclude that Kwanzaa simply is a "black Christmas."[4] One black critic of Kwanzaa stated recently that Kwanzaa's "rejectionist nature" makes the holiday "more about thumbing black noses at white America than about embracing the lost cause of resuming our Africanness."[5]

HISTORICAL CONTEXT

Cultural assimilation by African Americans has been a concern since the population of African slaves reached a critical mass in colonial America. In fact, slaveowners adopted policies of assimilation for their slaves that some observers today argue continue to impact the manner of black speech and culture. One of those policies was the common tactic of mixing an individual plantation's population of Africans so that members of a particular ethnic group did not dominate their respective slave quarter. Designed to minimize resistance and rebellion, this strategy forced the ethnically diverse slave populations in each region to develop a lingua franca, or common language, that would allow them to communicate. The result was a variation of English that borrowed elements from prominent West African languages such as Hausa, Yoruba, Wolof, and Bantu; collectively, in some parts of the slave South and throughout the Caribbean, this "black English" became known as Creole.

The same phenomenon happened with cultural traditions. Meshing elements of specific African cultures with the European traditions imposed on them by their masters, African and African American slaves developed a strategy of cultural blending, or creolization, that helped them create stronger connections within their individual communities. What emerged by the nineteenth century, of course, was a truly African American culture: one that had been created in the New World but borrowed heavily from West African cultures. Though emancipation changed the legal and political status of African Americans, those traditions of community bonds as a form of resistance to white power remained.

Two prominent African American leaders of the postslavery period, W.E.B. Du Bois and Booker T. Washington, adopted competing positions on the issue of assimilation. On one hand, Washington contended that only through acceptance of an inferior social and political status—and, by extension, through conceding the distinctive elements of their culture—could African Americans establish the patronage relationships with whites that might lead to equality of opportunity. On the other hand, Du Bois maintained that agitation and protest—as well as cultural distinctiveness—could eventually raise the social, political, and economic standing of black Americans. Though Du Bois and Washington were striving for the same goal, their differences on assimilation serve as the first prominent example of the debate that this chapter explores.[6]

By the 1920s, the premature death of Washington led to the Du Bois position becoming more popular. This converged with the Great Migration, which was a mass migration of African Americans from the South to northern cities, where economic and social opportunities beckoned. The result was the Harlem Renaissance, a cultural flowering of African American society that projected an image not only of distinctiveness but of equality with white culture. Black artists, authors, and musicians of the period—such as Palmer Hayden, Countee Cullen, Langston Hughes, and Roland Hayes—all celebrated African American culture while depicting the often-sobering realities of black life in America. The culmination of the Harlem Renaissance was the New Negro Movement, which was the first powerful assertion by African Americans of their individuality from white culture.

Though the Harlem Renaissance and New Negro Movement elicited significant criticisms by both blacks and whites, the evolution of black culture as a separate entity from white culture continued. In particular, the next logical step was a call for completely black separatism, which came first from Marcus Garvey in the 1920s. Promoting a black nationalism that transcended the boundaries of the United States, Garvey emphasized black racial identity as a source of pride. Though some of Garvey's financial endeavors ended in failure, he succeeded in developing subsequent generations of opponents to cultural assimilation by African Americans.

Those ideological descendants of Marcus Garvey reached their own apex during the civil rights movement of the 1960s. Though the political and legal side of the movement was dominated by more moderate activists like Martin Luther King Jr., a significant segment of the African American civil rights movement included black separatists like Malcolm X and Stokely Carmichael, who coined the term Black Power as a shorthand phrase for describing the unaccommodating spirit that some African Americans had adopted by the late 1960s.

Though the Watts race riot of 1966 radicalized some of these activists to the point of advocating violence, the late 1960s and early 1970s was a period of transition from activism to academic writing. In addition to the creation of Kwanzaa in 1966, Ebonics was first coined during this transitory period. Combining the words *ebony* and *phonics,* sociologist Robert L. Williams began promoting "black English" as a linguistically proper dialect of standard English. In 1975, his publication of *Ebonics: The True Language of Black Folks* moved the debate of cultural assimilation back into classrooms, newspaper offices, and even living rooms. The debates of the last 20 years, while naturally adopting forms specific to the times, roughly follow the original disagreement between Booker T. Washington, advocate of assimilation, and W.E.B. Du Bois, ardent opponent.[7]

Ebonics

When the Oakland, California, Board of Education created the Task Force on the Education of African American Students, none of its members could imagine the maelstrom that would soon ensue. In a school district in which 53 percent of students were African American, the Oakland school board was attempting to find ways to raise the level of education attainment by those students. Commissioned with finding potential solutions, the task force reported its conclusions to the full school board in late 1996. Though the plan was comprehensive, one component of the plan—recognizing Ebonics— became the center of the storm.

The task force's report, which became the subject of considerable scrutiny, sought recognition of Ebonics not only for what it saw as the betterment of black students, but also because the approval of Ebonics as a "second language" might make the Oakland school board eligible for much-needed federal funds earmarked for bilingual education. This theory—that recognizing Ebonics could make local school districts eligible for federal money designed to increase the numbers of English-speaking students—had garnered significant attention in the 1970s.[8] The school board was wary of the potential public relations backlash directed at both the recognition of Ebonics and the perception that such recognition was merely an attempt to receive more federal education money. Nonetheless, on December 18, 1996, members voted unanimously to accept the task force's recommendations.[9] In less than 48 hours, the Oakland decision became the premier national controversy of late 1996 and early 1997. Newspaper editorials, radio shows, and politicians all decried the decision, arguing that it was an affront to both standard English and American public education.[10]

Even some of the most prominent African American leaders challenged the wisdom of the Oakland resolution. Jesse Jackson, Maya Angelou, and Kweisi Mfume all argued that black students needed to learn standard English in order to participate fully as citizens. This argument within the black community regarding proper language was nothing new: in the early twentieth century, African American historian Carter Woodson observed that it had always been easy to find blacks who "scoff[ed] at the Negro dialect as some peculiar possession of the Negro which they should despise."[11] But, with even prominent African Americans depicting Ebonics as slang, the overwhelming reaction by the American public was that teaching Ebonics was wrong and that black Americans needed to do a better job of assimilating into American culture.

The public backlash spurred a quick unraveling of the Oakland school board's plans. Just days after the district's decision, the U.S. Department of Education diminished any hope of Ebonics instruction qualifying for federal bilingual money. "Elevating 'black English' to the status of a language," announced Education Secretary Richard W. Riley, "is not the way to raise standards of achievement in our schools and for our students. The Administration's policy is that 'Ebonics' is a non-standard form of English and not a foreign language." Though some linguists disagreed with Riley's depiction of Ebonics, the public opposition to the Oakland decision prevented any further positive action. In May 1997, the Oakland school board revisited the decision and omitted any reference to Ebonics in the task force's final report.[12]

The issue of Ebonics, however, has not faded as an historical issue. Many linguists and sociologists still contend that Ebonics, or what they prefer to call African American Vernacular English (AAVE), is a bona fide dialect of standard English. Researching in pockets of the South where African American communities were founded during Reconstruction, these social scientists maintain that strong linkages exist between modern black vernacular English and that of the nineteenth century.[13] As a tangible example of slavery's legacy, therefore, the issue of Ebonics illuminates the central arguments of the cultural assimilation debate.

FRAMING THE ISSUE

Often using Ebonics and Kwanzaa as concrete examples of the larger issue of African American culture meshing with American culture, both supporters and opponents of assimilation have developed pointed analyses of the issue. Supporters of cultural assimilation argue that because there is a tradition in American society of minority ethnic groups melding with the whole, African Americans should not be an exception. The most sophisticated advocates of this position base this argument not on any rejection of African Americans taking pride in their cultural traditions, but in what they see as African Americans' rejection of national culture. Both white and black assimilation supporters maintain that cultural separatism helps to perpetuate social divisions between American society and black members of that society.

Assimilation opponents, on the other hand, argue that the only way to maintain some semblance of African American identity and culture is to advocate traditions such as Ebonics and Kwanzaa that reach into their African past. Influenced considerably by the renewed interest in the African roots of black Americans, assimilation opponents contend that advocates of assimilation echo arguments of slaveowners and nineteenth-century social scientists, who argued fervently that African American traditions did not qualify as "culture." Indeed, although the debate over assimilation has evolved since the nineteenth century, its past of racial overtones still colors the modern controversy. An examination of the most salient aspects of each position reflects the sensitivity of each side to that unsavory earlier debate.

SUPPORTERS OF CULTURAL ASSIMILATION

Proponents of cultural assimilation by African Americans begin with an acceptance of black culture as an important element of American national culture but reject the claim that it is good for that black culture to be separate from national society. In essence, supporters hold on to the long-held notion of the nation as a melting pot, where various cultures offer different elements to the always-evolving national culture. Though this idea has been challenged in recent years, a significant number of Americans still hold the idea as an important goal of American civilization. Not surprisingly, this group constitutes the main supporters of cultural assimilation by African Americans.[14] Assimilation supporters also express concern that perpetuating separatist traditions such as Ebonics and Kwanzaa serves only to deepen the racial and ethnic divides that the United States continues to confront. Placing the onus on African Americans, assimilation supporters are a broadly diverse cross-section of the nation's ethnic groups. Two of the most prominent supporters, entertainer Bill Cosby and scholar John McWhorter, are African Americans, a point that underscores the internal tensions over assimilation among blacks in the United States.

Bill Cosby

In May 2004, Bill Cosby stepped away from his well-known position as the most successful African American television personality in America and into the energized assimilation debate. At an education forum in Washington, D.C., that had been organized to coincide with the 50th anniversary of the *Brown v. Board of Education* desegregation decision, Cosby leveled stinging criticism against African Americans who refused to alter their lives, behavior, and culture to fit the national culture. Focusing particularly on education problems linked to poverty, Cosby called for African Americans to stop making excuses for their plight and to start taking responsibility for their lives and actions. Remarking about inner-city blacks, Cosby said, "They're standing on the corner and they can't speak English. I can't even talk the way these people talk: 'Why you ain't,' 'Where you is' ... And I blamed the kid until I heard the mother talk. And then I heard the father talk." Concluding that efforts to recognize Ebonics would simply perpetuate these problems rather than help them, Cosby entered the debate on black cultural assimilation with a splash.[15]

Given the heated rhetoric between the two sides on this issue, Cosby soon found himself in the middle of both positive and negative reactions to his comments. NAACP Legal Defense and Education Fund president Theodore Shaw, who spoke at the forum immediately after Cosby, later observed that he changed his own remarks to soften the sting of Cosby's pointed commentary.[16] Other critics, such as Syl Jones, were not as generous as Shaw. "Cosby ... is a hypocrite of the first magnitude," Jones wrote in the aftermath of the entertainer's comments. "His early comedic performances featured black characters who spoke nonstandard English, wore ridiculous clothing and generally played the fool. His popular "Cosby Kids" cartoon show immortalized the eccentricities of black children.... In fact, Cosby practically invented the media image of the idiosyncratic black child."[17] And, in an irony not lost on many, the man whose *Cosby Show* portrayed an African American family as being part of American society had now become a major proponent of all African Americans assimilating into that society.

But, to the surprise of many observers, several prominent African Americans defended his remarks, arguing that it was past due for black Americans to assimilate fully into American society. Noted historian Henry Louis Gates Jr. recently defended Cosby's statements about Ebonics, arguing that "it isn't a derogation of the black vernacular—a marvelously rich and inventive tongue—to point out that there's a language of the marketplace, too, and learning to speak that language has generally been a precondition for economic success, whoever you are. When we let black youth become monolingual, we've limited their imaginative and economic possibilities."[18] Touching the nerve of both supporters and opponents of assimilation, Bill Cosby offered a stinging depiction of the problems inherent in conscious cultural separatism.

John McWhorter

Other pro-assimilation activists have been involved in the debate longer than Cosby, and in far less public venues. Nonetheless, the primary proponent is John McWhorter, a senior fellow at the Manhattan Institute and linguistics professor at the University of California at Berkeley. The author of three books on African American society, McWhorter focuses on the problems facing black Americans if cultural assimilation does not occur. In particular, McWhorter exhorts black Americans to use standard English, arguing that Ebonics is merely a dialect and an "excuse" not to assimilate fully into American society.[19]

McWhorter even challenges the usage of the term *African American*—instead of his preferred term, *black*—as a subtle but important lack of assimilation. "We are not African to any meaningful extent, but we are not white either,"

McWhorter explains. "The term 'African American' ... sets us apart from the mainstream. To term ourselves as part 'African' reinforces a sad implication: that our history is basically slave ships, plantations, lynching, fire hoses in Birmingham, and then South Central, and that we need to look back to Mother Africa to feel good about ourselves."[20] Arguing that the progress that African Americans have made from those institutions of oppression ought to make them proud to integrate their culture with the larger society, McWhorter remains a leading advocate for assimilation.

Finally, supporters of assimilation argue that efforts to create a separate black identity halt progress toward racial harmony. Some critics go so far as to suggest that efforts spent on promoting Ebonics and Kwanzaa would be more effective if they were spent on returning to the integrationist efforts of civil rights leaders such as Martin Luther King Jr. In this vein, a recent London *Times* story on Kwanzaa concluded that, given all of the problems of poverty, education, and leadership among African Americans, "the feast of Kwanzaa is a meaningless distraction.... Celebrating Kwanzaa once a year behind closed doors is far easier than reviving the corpse of the equal rights movement."[21]

OPPONENTS OF CULTURAL ASSIMILATION

Those opposed to cultural assimilation argue, first and foremost, that African Americans, like any other social and ethnic group, have the right to maintain a distinctive identity that does not mesh with the larger national culture. In essence, they reject the notion of the American "melting pot," by which all of the various ethnicities in the country eventually mold together into one—and, some assimilation opponents argue, decidedly white and European—culture. Viewing their position as an attempt to hold onto the positive aspects of an oppressive past, black assimilation opponents reject that black Americans must abandon many of their cultural traditions for the better of the whole.[22]

Much of this argument rests on the impact of slavery on African Americans. Aside from the reparations debate, discussed in chapter 1, the debate over assimilation examines the long-term cultural effects of enslavement. In particular, some assimilation opponents contend that the characterization of the Ebonics debate smacks of slavery; in the same way that slaveowners held that slaves had no proper language, these opponents say modern American society is relegating a linguistically sound dialect to the status of a bastardized version of white English. Moreover, these assimilation critics point out, the very existence of Ebonics grew out of the enslavement of Africans and African Americans by white Europeans and Americans. In that sense, then, the assimilation debate takes on decidedly similar overtones to the reparations debate;

how each side interprets the historical context, therefore, is a key issue in determining which argument is persuasive.

Maulana Karenga

The founder of Kwanzaa remains an instrumental figure in the opposition to cultural assimilation by African Americans. Born Ron Everett, Maulana Karenga adopted an African-based identity as a result of his participation in the radical wing of the civil rights movement. As a Black Panther and contemporary of Malcolm X, Karenga developed his activism in the separatist, black nationalist tradition of Marcus Garvey. Since the 1970s, Karenga has served as chair of the Black Studies Department at the California State University, Long Beach. He is also the founder of The Organization Us, an organization that promotes the African basis for black American culture. Rooted in Marcus Garvey's ideas of pan-Africanism, or solidarity of all African-descended peoples regardless of where they live, The Organization Us is dedicated "to continuing the cultural revolution initiated in the 1960s," which is accomplished by "sustaining and always expanding and deepening the dialog with African culture."[23]

Building upon the increasing popularity of Kwanzaa, Maulana Karenga has devoted significant efforts to the creation of his doctrine of Kawaida, which is what he describes as "an ongoing synthesis of the best of African thought and practice in constant exchange with the world."[24] Perhaps even more rooted in African cultures than Kwanzaa, Kawaida may be an even greater rejection of cultural assimilation. One follower of the doctrine explains it precisely in that context: "The essential importance of Karenga's Doctrine of Kawaida is that it lays out a 'Black Value System' as a guide to our behavior toward each other and in our pursuit of achieving liberation and strong communities and nations. Emulating the values of those who have oppressed us and creating structures based on these values is a prescription for continued stagnation and underdevelopment."[25]

Currently, as Maulana Karenga's leadership of the anti-assimilation movement illustrates, the most effective opponents of cultural assimilation are scholars, who have made quiet but effective inroads in returning the assimilation debate to research studies. In particular, Ebonics has benefited from this turn. Social scientists Robin Means Coleman and Jack L. Daniel recently concluded, "The issue of Ebonics, it seems, has become one of racial politics where that which is associated with Blackness is distorted and caricatured to the absurd." Reviewing the major news stories on the Oakland matter, Coleman and Daniels illustrate what they claim is a pattern of skewed coverage that is not only incorrect, but harmful. This type of coverage, they argue, delays the important debate over whether the recognition of Ebonics by other school districts would actually be a good strategy for educating African American students. "By approaching Ebonics from the absurd," Coleman and Daniels argue, the "media failed to acknowledge two key issues: First, the relevance of the historical, linguistic roots of Ebonics—slavery, and second, the need for aggressive, improved education efforts for African American children."[26]

In sum, the opposing argument maintains that modern African Americans, in moving out of the shadow of slavery, have promoted unique cultural traditions that give them pride, rather than shame, in their past. But the characterization of Ebonics, and to a lesser extent, Kwanzaa, as improper cultural expressions merely confirms what most of the assimilation opponents already argue: that the very people arguing for black Americans to give up these traditions are those who consider black culture as offering very little to the melting pot. As long as the two sides cannot reach some common ground, the debate over cultural assimilation will rage well into the twenty-first century.

QUESTIONS AND ACTIVITIES

1. What does cultural assimilation entail? What is the historical background for the debate over cultural assimilation?

2. How is the modern debate over assimilation similar to the debate between W.E.B. Du Bois and Booker T. Washington?

3. What is Ebonics? What are the arguments of its proponents and detractors? Should it be recognized as an official dialect of standard English?

4. What is Kwanzaa? What are the seven principles that govern the celebration? Can you see elements of both African and Western cultures in Kwanzaa?

5. Organize your class into two groups—one side should adopt the position of assimilation supporters, while the other should adopt the position of opponents. Debate the issue. What are the most persuasive arguments of each side?

6. Are there other examples in American society of dialects like Ebonics? If so, are there similar debates over assimilation that involve the people who speak those dialects?

7. What is the idea of the "melting pot"? The "salad bowl"? Which of these is a more accurate portrayal of American society and why?

8. What other ethnic groups in the United States face similar questions of assimilation?

9. Why has the assimilation debate focused so much on African Americans?

NOTES

1. Also Bree, "What Is Kwanzaa?" *Black Voices,* http://www.blackvoices.com/feature/kwanzaa/.

2. Ysamur Flores-Peña and Robin Evanchuk, "Kwanzaa: The Emergence of an African-American Holiday," *Western Folklore* 56 (1997): 281.

3. Ylonda Gault Caviness, "The Spirit of Kwanzaa," *Essence,* December 2002.

4. Elizabeth Pleck, "Kwanzaa: The Making of a Black Nationalist Tradition, 1966–1990," *Journal of American Ethnic History* 20 (2001): 3–28.

5. Debra J. Dickerson, "A Case of the Kwanzaa Blues," *New York Times,* 26 December 2003.

6. Cary D. Wintz, ed, *African American Political Thought, 1890–1930: Washington, Du Bois, Garvey, and Randolph* (Armonk, New York: Sharpe, 1996).

7. Robert L. Williams, *Ebonics: The True Language of Black Folks* (St. Louis: Institute of Black Studies, 1975).

8. Harry N. Seymour and Charlena M. Seymour, "Ebonics and Public Law 94–142," *Journal of Black Studies* 9 (1979): 449–68.

9. Lori Olszewski, "Oakland Schools OK Black English," *San Francisco Chronicle,* 19 December 1996.

10. Nanette Asimov and Lori Olszewski, "Black English Decision Hits National Nerve," *San Francisco Chronicle,* 20 December 1996.

11. Carter G. Woodson, *Mis-education of the Negro* (New York: AMS Press, 1977), 619.

12. Peter Applebome, "'Ebonics' Omitted in Oakland Report on Teaching English," *New York Times,* 6 May 1997.

13. Walt Wolfram and Erik R. Thomas, *The Development of African American English* (Malden, Mass.: Blackwell, 2002).

14. Michael Barone, *The New Americans: How the Melting Pot Can Work Again* (Washington, D.C.: Regnery Books, 2001).

15. Manny Fernandez, "Cosby Defends Criticism of Black Community; Actor Urges Better Parenting at Education Forum in D.C.," *Washington Post,* 9 September 2004.

16. Theodore M. Shaw, "Beyond What Cosby Said," *Washington Post,* 27 May 2004.

17. Syl Jones, "Cosby Once Was Part of the Problem; Yet He Could Do Much More to Work toward Solution," *Minneapolis Star Tribune,* 8 August 2004.

18. Henry Louis Gates Jr., "Breaking the Silence," *New York Times,* 1 August 2004.

19. John H. McWhorter, *Doing Our Own Thing: The Degradation of Language and Music and Why We Should, Like, Care* (New York: Gotham Books, 2003).

20. John McWhorter, "Why I'm Black, Not African American," 9 September 2004, *RealClearPolitics* Commentary, http://www.realclearpolitics.com/Commentary/com-9_9_04_McWhorter.html.

21. Nicholas Wapshott, "African Americans Have Little to Toast at Kwanzaa," *Times* (London), 29 December 2003.

22. William Booth, "One Nation, Indivisible: Is It History," *The Myth of the Melting Pot,* Washingtonpost.com, 22 February 1998, http://www.washingtonpost.com/wp-srv/national/longterm/meltingpot/melt0222.htm.

23. "Philosophy, Principles, Program," The Organization Us Web Site, http://www.us-organization.org/30th/ppp.html.

24. "Kwanzaa: A Celebration of Family, Community, and Culture," *The Official Kwanzaa Web site,* February 1997, http://www.officialkwanzaawebsite.org/karengabio.html.

25. Ron Daniels, "Reconstructing Nations," *Carolina Peacemaker,* 22–28 January 2004, 7A.

26. Robin R. Means Coleman and Jack L. Daniel, "Mediating Ebonics," *Journal of Black Studies* 31 (2000): 82, 91.

SUGGESTED READING

Applebome, Peter. "'Ebonics' Omitted in Oakland Report on Teaching English." *New York Times,* 6 May 1997.

Asimov, Nanette, and Lori Olszewski. "Black English Decision Hits National Nerve." *San Francisco Chronicle,* 20 December 1996.

Barone, Michael. *The New Americans: How the Melting Pot Can Work Again.* Washington, D.C.: Regnery Books, 2001.

Booth, William. "One Nation, Indivisible: Is It History." *The Myth of the Melting Pot,* Washingtonpost.com, 22 February 1998, http://www.washingtonpost. com/wp-srv/national/longterm/meltingpot/melt0222.htm.

Bree, Also. "What Is Kwanzaa?" *Black Voices,* http://www.blackvoices.com/feature/ kwanzaa/.

Caviness, Ylonda Gault. "The Spirit of Kwanzaa." *Essence,* December 2002.

Coleman, Robin R. Means, and Jack L. Daniel. "Mediating Ebonics." *Journal of Black Studies* 31 (2000): 74–95.

Daniels, Ron. "Reconstructing Nations." *Carolina Peacemaker,* 22–28 January 2004.

Dickerson, Debra J. *The End of Blackness: Returning the Souls of Black Folk to Their Rightful Owners.* New York: Pantheon Books, 2004.

Fernandez, Manny. "Cosby Defends Criticism of Black Community; Actor Urges Better Parenting at Education Forum in D.C." *Washington Post,* 9 September 2004.

Flores-Peña, Ysamur, and Robin Evanchuk. "Kwanzaa: The Emergence of an African-American Holiday." *Western Folklore* 56 (1997): 281–94.

Gates, Henry Louis Jr. "Breaking the Silence." *New York Times,* 1 August 2004.

Jones, Syl. "Cosby Once Was Part of the Problem; Yet He Could Do Much More to Work Toward Solution." *Minneapolis Star Tribune,* 8 August 2004.

Karenga, Maulana. *The African American Holiday of Kwanzaa: A Celebration of Family, Community and Culture.* Los Angeles: University of Sankore Press, 1988.

McWhorter, John H. *Doing Our Own Thing: The Degradation of Language and Music and Why We Should, Like, Care.* New York: Gotham Books, 2003.

———. "Why I'm Black, Not African American," 9 September 2004, *RealClearPolitics,* http://www.realclearpolitics.com/Commentary/com_9_04_McWhorter.html.

Olszewski, Lori. "Oakland Schools OK Black English," *San Francisco Chronicle,* 19 December 1996.

Pleck, Elizabeth. "Kwanzaa: The Making of a Black Nationalist Tradition, 1966–1990." *Journal of American Ethnic History* 20 (2001): 3–28.

Seymour, Harry N., and Charlena M. Seymour. "Ebonics and Public Law 94–142." *Journal of Black Studies* 9 (1979): 449–68.

Shaw, Theodore M. "Beyond What Cosby Said." *Washington Post,* 27 May 2004.

Wapshott, Nicholas. "African Americans Have Little to Toast at Kwanzaa." *Times* (London), 29 December 2003.

Williams, Robert L. *Ebonics: The True Language of Black Folks.* St. Louis: Institute of Black Studies, 1975.

Wintz, Cary D., ed. *African American Political Thought, 1890–1930: Washington, Du Bois, Garvey, and Randolph*. Armonk, New York: Sharpe, 1996.

Wolfram, Walt, and Erik R. Thomas. *The Development of African American English*. Malden, Mass.: Blackwell, 2002.

Woodson, Carter G. *Mis-education of the Negro*. New York: AMS Press, 1977.

Videos

Kwanzaa—African American History: Vol. I. Bonneville Video, 1998.

Kwanzaa (Holidays for Children Series). Schlessinger Media, 1994.

The MEE Kwanzaa Video. Motivational Educational Entertainment, http://www. meeproductions.com/store/kwanzaa.cfm. *The MEE Kwanzaa Video* follows four characters as they celebrate Kwanzaa in different settings with the people close to them. It explains the seven principles of Kwanzaa and the various ceremonial items. The video provides a entertaining addition to any Kwanzaa celebration.

Web Sites

Ebonics Information Page, Center for Applied Linguistics, http://www.cal.org/ ebonics.

The Official Kwanzaa Web Site, http://www.officialkwanzaawebsite.org.

The Organization Us, http://www.us-organization.org.

4

AFFIRMATIVE ACTION

"It is not enough just to open the gates of opportunity," President Lyndon B. Johnson remarked in 1965. "All our citizens must have the ability to walk through those gates." Speaking at Howard University's commencement ceremonies, the president was stoking support for the Voting Rights Act that would eventually be passed by Congress in August 1965. Aside from African American voting rights, however, Johnson's historic speech also addressed the issue of affirmative action, which was still a nascent idea and federal policy. Pointing to that possibility in future congressional and executive action, Johnson remarked, "We seek not just freedom but opportunity. We seek not just legal equity but human ability, not just equality as a right and a theory but equality as a fact and equality as a result."[1] Just two months after the address, and shortly after Congress passed the Voting Rights Act of 1965, President Johnson issued an executive order mandating affirmative action in federal contracting.

As a result of his speech and subsequent executive order, Lyndon Johnson waded into the increasingly controversial issue of affirmative action. While his comments and policy action focused on affirmative action in hiring, another important arena in which affirmative action has become both formal policy and political controversy is university admissions. Thus, this chapter explores affirmative action in both employment and education. Supporters of affirmative action contend that the policy helps to correct past injustices by ensuring equality of access to universities and equality of opportunity in employment. Opponents argue that affirmative action emphasizes skin color over skills, which, in their words, is "reverse discrimination." In the early twenty-first century, the debate over affirmative action has centered on its necessity and effectiveness 40 years after its introduction as formal policy. Moreover, supporters and opponents dispute even the very definition of affirmative action, which indicates the level of dispute this issue elicits from activists on both sides. By examining each position in detail, this chapter will offer a comprehensive understanding of why affirmative action is such an important issue in modern American society.

HISTORICAL CONTEXT

Although the term *affirmative action* is a relatively new addition to the American lexicon, the idea is one that has evolved since Reconstruction. Radical Republican leaders, in creating agencies such as the Freedmen's Bureau, attempted to create equal access to fundamental rights such as education and marriage, both of which had been illegal for slaves. Even the still-born proposal for "40 acres and a mule" (discussed in chapter 1) addressed what observers today would view as equal access to economic gain. Thus, even though politicians and leaders of the Reconstruction era used very different terminology than what modern activists in the affirmative action debate employ, they did lay the groundwork for the evolution of the issue.

No better example for that idea exists than the ratification of the 14th Amendment in 1868. The culmination of many Radicals' efforts to secure constitutional protection of basic civil rights for African Americans, the amendment necessarily addressed the immediate concerns of the late 1860s. But since that time, the 14th Amendment has become one of the most important components of the Constitution in American jurisprudence. Of the five sections of the 14th Amendment, the most significant, at least for the issue of African American civil rights, is the first:

> All persons born or naturalized in the United States, and subject to the jurisdiction thereof, are citizens of the United States and of the State wherein they reside. No State shall abridge the privileges or immunities of citizens of the United States; nor shall any State deprive any person of life, liberty, or property, without due process of law; nor deny to any person within its jurisdiction the equal protection of the laws.

As the grounds upon which many civil rights cases rested, the amendment is often the subject of competing interpretations by supporters and opponents of affirmative action. On the one hand, supporters argue that the amendment provides the federal government the constitutional means to correct past injustices by states, individuals, and even the federal government itself;

affirmative action, supporters argue, is the modern means of fulfilling the spirit of the amendment. Opponents, on the other hand, argue that affirmative action, in displacing potential employees or students who are not African American, violates the amendment.

Prior to becoming the subject of scrutiny by people involved in the modern affirmative action debate, the 14th Amendment helped to spur the evolution of federal policy toward affirmative action. In 1896, in what would later be viewed as a decision that stunted that evolution, the U.S. Supreme Court dictated a policy of "separate but equal" in *Plessy v. Ferguson*. Aimed at ensuring equal access to schools, public facilities, and private establishments such as restaurants, the decision also required that such equality be segregated according to race. Moreover, with states ultimately responsible for enforcing the decision, the *Plessy* case ensured only the "separate"—not the "equal"—portion of the policy. As a result, early-twentieth-century civil rights leaders pushed for federal action that would correct this inequality.

One ironic aspect of the *Plessy* decision was that, by affirming a policy of de facto inequality for several more decades, it furthered the race-based injustice that later leaders would use to justify an affirmative action policy. The first time that the phrase "affirmative action" was used in government policy, however, it did not refer to African Americans. Instead, in the 1935 Wagner Act, the phrase pertained to union organizers and union members whose employers had engaged in unfair labor practices. Requiring those employers to take "affirmative action" by reinstating unionized employees, the Wagner Act corrected antiunion sentiment and, more importantly for the history of affirmative action for African Americans, created the precedent for government intervention into private business for the purpose of repairing a legal and social problem.[2]

In 1941, using that precedent, President Franklin Roosevelt issued Executive Order 8802, which declared that the federal government would "encourage full participation in the national defense program by all citizens of the United States, regardless of race, creed, color, or national origin." Spurred to action by the black union leader A. Philip Randolph, Roosevelt subtly advanced the cause of nondiscrimination in public and private hiring. On the eve of American entry into World War II, the president's policy skirted the legislative power of Congress, in which such a policy would not have received a majority. In fact, as subsequent examples will illustrate, the practice of presidents issuing executive orders regarding the issue of affirmative action would become very common until, in the late 1960s, a majority of members of Congress had warmed to the policy. In addition, like future executive orders, Roosevelt's created a presidential commission, in this case the Fair Employment Practice Committee, to ensure enforcement of the new policy.[3]

In the 1950s, two fundamental decisions—one executive and one judicial—accelerated the move toward a formal, comprehensive affirmative action policy. In 1953, Roosevelt's successor, Harry Truman, created the Committee on Government Contract Compliance, which was an effort to expand further federal oversight of nondiscrimination in government contract jobs. In its report that year, the committee directed the Bureau of Employment Security "to act positively and affirmatively to implement the policy of nondiscrimination."[4] The next year, and much more prominently, the U.S. Supreme Court, in its *Brown v. Board of Education* decision, overturned the "separate but equal" policy of the *Plessy* case. Simultaneously eroding segregation and building momentum toward a proactive, "affirmative" strategy of correcting generations of discrimination, the *Brown* decision, based largely on the 14th Amendment, was a landmark for civil rights generally.

As with most issues involving African American civil rights efforts, the 1960s was the watershed decade for action. In 1961, under pressure from civil rights leaders such as Martin Luther King Jr., President John Kennedy issued Executive Order 10925 creating the President's Committee on Equal Employment Opportunity. Kennedy charged the committee "to consider and recommend additional affirmative steps which should be taken by executive departments and agencies to realize more fully the national policy of nondiscrimination within the executive branch." Moreover, the president declared, contractors with the federal government had to agree to "take affirmative action to ensure that applicants are employed, and that employees are treated" without regard to their race. While significant in increasing the federal government's role in ending nondiscrimination, Executive Order 10925 did not quite adopt the definition of affirmative action as a proactive policy to hire minority candidates.[5]

That fundamental change in definition came in 1964, in legislation passed by Congress, and in 1965, in executive action by Kennedy's successor, Lyndon Johnson. The Civil Rights Act of 1964, seen by many historians as the true culmination of Reconstruction (which formally ended in 1877), cemented all the executive, judicial, and legislative policies on nondiscrimination up to that point. But it also opened the door to another possibility: once nondiscrimination was the law of the land, what could be done to repair the damage done by centuries of enslavement, segregation, and discrimination? According to one section of the Civil Rights Act, the court system could order "affirmative action"—such as reinstatement, or hiring, of employees who had experienced discriminatory action by an employer. While a step forward in correcting race-based discrimination, this policy was still reactionary in that it addressed problems only after the fact. Thus, in his June 1965 speech at Howard University, President Johnson set the stage for the redefining of affirmative action as a proactive, rather than reactive, policy.

The formal policy came in the form of Johnson's Executive Order 11246, issued in September 1965. As the most important executive order up to that point, and since, on the matter of affirmative action, it was, literally and figuratively, a defining event in the history of the issue. Focusing on federal contractors as a means of penetrating private entities, the policy went beyond Kennedy's earlier policy by requiring "affirmative action" in all parts of a contractor's operations, not just those directly involved with the government. The meat of the order was in its first clause:

> The contractor will not discriminate against any employee or applicant for employment because of race, color, religion, sex, or national origin. The contractor will take affirmative action to ensure that applicants are employed, and that employees are treated during employment, without regard to their race, color, religion, sex or national origin. Such action shall include, but not be limited to the following: employment, upgrading, demotion, or transfer; recruitment or recruitment advertising; layoff or termination; rates of pay or other forms of compensation; and selection for training, including apprenticeship.[6]

The penalties for failing to comply with the order were (and are) not only termination of the existing contract and ineligibility for bidding on future contracts, but also judicial proceedings based on the Civil Rights Act of 1964. Thus, after generations of working toward a formal, federal policy of non-discrimination and affirmative action, civil rights leaders and their politician allies found victory in President Johnson's policy.

This, of course, was not the end of the issue. In addition to severe reaction against the policy, which still exists today, supporters of affirmative action sought additional measures. In particular, the imposition of numerical goals, or quotas, was seen as an important gauge of how effective this new policy would be. Thus, in 1967, President Johnson amended his original order not only to include women, but also to set quantified goals of minority and female employees for employers. In 1969 and 1970, the Labor Department expanded this directive further by requiring federal contractors with 50 or more employees and a contract of $50,000 or more to submit annual reports on their affirmative action plans. This so-called Philadelphia Plan, although challenged in court, remained in effect when the Supreme Court decided against reviewing the case.[7]

Though all of the federal action on affirmative action had been focused on employment practices, many universities adopted the policies of affirmative action and quotas during the 1970s. The dramatic increase in government contractors, employees, and college students who were African American came as a direct result of affirmative action. While civil rights leaders applauded this progress, however, others were beginning to question what they saw as valuing one racial group's interests above those of others.

In 1978, this anti–affirmative action sentiment culminated in a landmark Supreme Court decision. The case, *Regents of the University of California v. Bakke,* considered the experience of Alan Bakke, a white man, who was denied admission to the University of California Medical School. Bakke maintained that the school's affirmative action and quota policy had produced a two-tiered admissions policy—one set of standards for whites and one set of standards for African Americans. In the most important pronouncement on affirmative action in its early history, the Supreme Court ruled that the medical school's admission policy was illegal and that Bakke must be admitted. But in the same ruling, an individual opinion by Justice Lewis Powell kept affirmative action alive. Justice Powell concluded that in some instances "the goal of achieving a diverse student body is sufficiently compelling to justify consideration of race in admissions decisions."[8] Thus, if affirmative action was used as a "plus factor," as opposed to producing a quota for minority students, it could remain. In short, then, the Supreme Court struck down the use of quotas but left room for affirmative action to remain in certain instances.[9] As a result, universities rushed to avoid the two-tiered policy that had drawn action by the court while maintaining race as a factor in admissions.

Since the *Bakke* decision, some of the highest-profile affirmative action controversies have involved state ballot initiatives. The best example of these is the 1996 initiative in California, Proposition 209. Authored by Ward Connerly, a black California businessman and member of the University of California Board of Regents, the proposed amendment to the California state constitution was a direct challenge to affirmative action. The first clause of the proposal states, "The state shall not discriminate against, or grant preferential treatment to, any individual or group on the basis of race, sex, color, ethnicity, or national origin in the operation of public employment, public education, or public contracting."[10] Governor Pete Wilson supported the proposal, which attracted significant attention nationally as an important test case for the apparently growing opposition to affirmative action. As a comprehensive assault on affirmative action, interest groups on both sides of the debate invested significant resources into the campaign.

When the polls closed on November 5, 1996, California voters passed Proposition 209 with 54 percent of the vote. Claiming a victory over the "obsessive concern about race," Ward Connerly held up the proposal as an example of his and others' interpretation of integration. Opponents were not impressed and vowed legal challenges. Charging that the proposal was "drafted in such a deceptive way," Aileen Hernandez, a former member of the U.S. Equal Employment Opportunity Commission, declared, "It's absolutely essential that we challenge this in court."[11]

Opponents of Prop 209 did challenge it in court. A flurry of cases questioned the constitutionality of the provision and rested on an interpretation of the 1964 Civil Rights Act that government had an obligation to make amends for discrimination. The cases wound through the federal courts until late 1997, when the U.S. Supreme Court refused to hear the case. Allowing a federal appeals court decision upholding the proposal to stand, the legal wrangling over the issue effectively ended. Governor Wilson placed an exclamation point on the victory secured by Prop 209 supporters: "It is time for those who have resisted Proposition 209 to acknowledge that equal rights under the law, not special preferences, is the law of the land."[12]

But the controversy was not quite over. Ronald Takaki, a historian at the University of California at Berkeley, then entered the debate after the courts refused to overturn Prop 209. In particular, in 1998 Takaki spearheaded a ballot initiative in California that was aimed at reinstituting affirmative action in the state. The so-called California Equality Initiative would have made legal the practice of considering race and gender in hiring and college admissions, though it would not have reinstated quotas.[13] In a testament to public opinion against affirmative action, Takaki's proposal did not even qualify for the state ballot. Since the late 1990s, in spite of numerous challenges, Proposition 209 remains law and has even been used recently to strike down city ordinances that violate the policy.[14]

Hopwood v. University of Texas Law School

In the legal arena, a similar set of circumstances to those of Alan Bakke produced the next significant legal challenge to affirmative action. Cheryl Hopwood, a white applicant to the University of Texas Law School, was denied admission. Claiming that the school's affirmative action policy prevented her from being admitted, Hopwood sued. In March 1996, the Fifth U.S. Circuit Court of Appeals struck down the affirmative action policy at the law school; because of the regional jurisdiction of the court, the ruling applied to all schools in Louisiana, Texas, and Oklahoma. In writing the decision for the court, Judge Jerry E. Smith did not accept the argument that affirmative action was designed to correct past injustices. He concluded, "A broad program that sweeps in all minorities with a remedy that is in no way related to past harms cannot survive constitutional scrutiny."[15]

But the court's decision was just the beginning of the Hopwood controversy. Admissions officials at the University of Texas, as well as state officials, felt powerless in the wake of the decision. "Every day of the week," Bruce Walker, director of admissions at the university, said, "I wake up wishing I could have affirmative action back. But this is the dish we got served, and

Supporters of Affirmative Action rally in front of the U.S. Supreme Court in Washington, D.C., in 2003 (AP Wide World Photo/Charles Dharapak).

we're making the best of it." In 1997, the Texas state legislature instituted a remedy, the so-called top 10 percent plan, which automatically admitted to any Texas state university high school students who finished in the top 10 percent of their class. Allowing colleges to attain broad diversity without the policy of affirmative action, the plan did result in a significant recovery in African American students at the University of Texas following a precipitous drop. But with most of the faculty supporting the return of affirmative action, and with most of the students and citizens in the state opposed, the issue certainly drove a wedge between groups on campus.[16] Prepared to deal with life after affirmative action, neither side expected that the next legal case involving the issue would be so significant.

Bollinger Cases

Much of the frustration over the Hopwood decision—for both supporters and opponents of affirmative action—came from the apparent lack of desire by the Supreme Court to revisit the issue. But on June 24, 2003, the Court finally acted. In reviewing two cases involving the University of Michigan—*Gratz v. Bollinger*, involving the university's undergraduate admissions policy, and *Grutter v. Bollinger*, involving the university's law school admissions process—the Court determined to make these cases the most recent pronouncements on the issue. Like the Bakke and Hopwood cases, the Michigan cases began with the claim by white applicants that they had been denied admission because of the school's affirmative action policy in admissions; also like its Bakke decision, the Supreme Court would render somewhat of a mixed endorsement of affirmative action.[17]

The Court considered each case against the University of Michigan separately, which resulted in separate rulings. In *Gratz*, the case involving the undergraduate school, a 6–3 majority struck down the university's mechanistic point system that awarded any minority applicant an automatic 20 points on a 150-point scale. The decision left open, however, the possibility that a tweaked alternative to the point system would be constitutional.[18]

The first case certainly received less attention than the *Grutter* decision. In a 5–4 majority, the Court upheld the law school's affirmative action policy. The absence of a quotalike system akin to the undergraduate school's admissions process allowed the Michigan Law School to withstand the Court's scrutiny. Justice Sandra Day O'Connor, who voted with the majority in each case, leaned heavily on the 1978 opinion of Justice Powell in the *Bakke* decision. She declared:

> Effective participation by members of all racial and ethnic groups in the civic life of our Nation is essential if the dream of one nation, indivisible, is to be realized. . . . Moreover, universities, and, in particular, law schools, represent the training ground for a large number of our Nation's leaders. In order to cultivate a set of leaders with legitimacy in the eyes of the citizenry, it is necessary that the path to leadership be visibly open to talented and qualified individuals of every race and ethnicity.[19]

The dissenting opinion was scathing. Calling the admissions policy a "sham" and a "naked effort to achieve racial balancing," Chief Justice William Rehnquist expressed dismay that the Court would allow affirmative action to continue.[20]

Supporters of affirmative action rejoiced. Mary Sue Coleman, president of the University of Michigan, declared, "This is a tremendous victory for the University of Michigan, for all of higher education, and for the hundreds of groups and individuals who supported us. A majority of the court has finally endorsed the principle of diversity."[21] Indeed, by providing both an endorsement of, and a clear plan for, affirmative action, the High Court seemed to provide at least temporary respite from the legal wrangling that had beset affirmative action in the late twentieth and early twenty-first centuries.

FRAMING THE ISSUE

As one of the most controversial public policy issues in the United States today, affirmative action draws vehement supporters and opponents. Wrapped up in the historical legacy of slavery and segregation, the policy of affirmative action typically divides activists and observers according to their perspective on whether modern American society ought to repair the wrongs of slavery and segregation. Supporters, therefore, base their arguments on the fundamental assumption that American society must continue to right those evils from the past. They also argue that because racism continues to exist—both in society generally and in specific situations such as hiring and college admissions—affirmative action must continue. Opponents, on the other hand, reject the claim that Americans today must continue to pay for slavery and segregation; moreover, critics of affirmative action argue that while the policy was appropriate for the 1960s and 1970s, it is no longer acceptable today, given the positive changes in racial attitudes that have occurred since that time. By exploring each position in detail, as well as the specific arguments of high-profile activists on each side, the fuller context of affirmative action will be clear.

SUPPORTERS OF AFFIRMATIVE ACTION

Affirmative action proponents base their position on four distinct arguments. First, they contend, because there is no debate that race-based discrimination existed in the United States, modern solutions to that problem must also be race-based. In other words, if an entire group was targeted negatively by institutionalized racism, modern society's remedy must also target that group. Second, proponents claim that whites have enjoyed, and continue to enjoy, unfair advantages in acquiring employment and being admitted to college. The last two arguments in favor of affirmative action center on its effects. Since the 1960s, supporters argue, affirmative action has created employment and educational opportunities for African Americans that were previously lacking, or even completely impossible for them to attain. The subsequent learning of skills has produced a growing black middle class, which is already inculcating new generations of African Americans with the expectation that those historically shut out jobs and colleges are, indeed, possible. Finally, in securing jobs and college slots for African Americans, affirmative action has helped to reduce racial stereotypes; consequently, the task of overcoming racist hurdles—particularly those in institutions—will be easier in the future.

The first of these central arguments of supporters, that the federal government must support and enforce a group-based remedy, is necessarily couched in historical terms. Generations of slaves, and then generations of fre[e] who could not vote, acquire college-level education, or, in some ca[se] leave the former plantation on which they worked, produced dee[p] long-term economic problems inherent in most black communities in the United States. Even the migration of millions of African Americans from the segregationist South during the interwar period did little to offset the economic and social problems created by discrimination. Thus, supporters contend, all one has to do to appreciate the tangible legacy of racism is to examine modern poverty rates among African Americans: the most recent data indicate that the black poverty rate remains nearly twice (24.4%) that of the national rate (12.5%).[22] In linking this modern problem with past, and even continuing, racism, supporters maintain that the only feasible solution is to target the affected group with policies such as affirmative action.

Without affirmative action, proponents argue, the historic advantage whites have enjoyed in acquiring jobs and being admitted to college would continue unabated. In fact, supporters point to data that indicate the continuation of that advantage if affirmative action is not in place. In the immediate aftermath of the Hopwood decision, for example, African American enrollment at the University of Texas and at Texas A&M University plummeted; eradicating race as an admissions factor was debilitating for admissions officers and university officials who worked diligently to produce an ethnically diverse student body. Even with new, "more aggressive and comprehensive recruitment activities as a major response to *Hopwood*," the number of first-time, entering African American freshmen at Texas's two major universities dropped 25 percent in 1997, the year after the Hopwood decision.[23] Supporters of affirmative action decried the effects of the decision and used those statistics in their legal and public responses to it.

Other data point to the positive effects that affirmative action has produced, supporters argue. Since the 1960s, when affirmative action was introduced, the percentage of African Americans with four-year college degrees has increased significantly. Figure 4.1 illustrates the increase clearly.[24]

In spite of those gains, however, African Americans are still underrepresented among all university students in the nation. A recent report by the U.S. Department of Education found that African Americans, while constituting 13 percent of the nation's population, account for only 11 percent of all college students. Rod Paige, U.S. Secretary of Education, himself African American, concluded, "Despite some gains, black children and adults don't advance to the next level at the same rate as our white peers." The increase in black degree earners, too, might not be as positive as it seems on the surface. "The situation would be much worse," Secretary Paige commented, "without our Historically Black Colleges and Universities, which continue to be

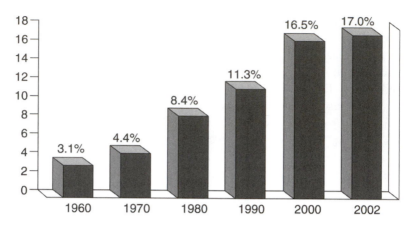

Figure 4.1   Percentage of all Black Adults Over the Age of 25 Who Held a Four-Year College Degree.

Source: U.S. Bureau of the Census. Chart copyright *The Journal of Blacks in Higher Education.*

extremely valuable, as can be evidenced by the fact that one-fourth of blacks in college are in HBCUs, and these institutions have produced some of our finest graduates and keenest minds."[25] Not lost on supporters of affirmative action, considerable pressure continues to be exerted to maintain the policy in college admissions.

Proponents of affirmative action also point to data on employment to underscore both the positive effect of the policy and the continuing need for it. Economist Barbara Bergmann cites a number of large companies and metropolitan areas where African American employees are considerably underrepresented. She argues, "In spite of the progress toward fair access that has been made since the 1960s, we are not even close to having achieved a labor market in which a candidate's sex and race don't matter." In Bergmann's estimation, the two government agencies designed to enforce affirmative action policies, the Equal Employment Opportunity Commission and the Office of Federal Contract Compliance Programs, are too underfunded and understaffed to conduct the number of reviews necessary to make considerable change. Thus, for Bergmann and other supporters of affirmative action, the problem is not just in the past, but very much in the present. Pointing to these limitations, Bergmann concludes, "We cannot expect a great deal of progress in integrating the workplace ... without a systematic program that pushes people to act differently. The purpose of affirmative action is to supply that push."[26]

Mary Frances Berry

One of the most vocal and influential supporters of affirmative action is Mary Frances Berry. Chairwoman of the U.S. Civil Rights Commission and professor of American social thought at the University of Pennsylvania, Berry has been active in the affirmative action debate since the early 1980s, when she first joined the commission. As a legal scholar and historian, Mary Frances Berry frequently uses the historical context of discrimination to elicit support for affirmative action. In the past, Berry observes, "What we had was preference for white men and to a large extent, it's still that way." As a leading figure in the fight against scaling back affirmative action, Berry argues, "Instead of less affirmative action, we need more. Some people say they don't like affirmative action because it doesn't help poor people, but affirmative action has helped pull people out of poverty, and it sends a beacon of hope for poor people that if they work hard they can get opportunity."[27]

In her position with the Civil Rights Commission, Berry has been involved primarily in workplace and voter discrimination (discussed in chapter 9) but does not miss opportunities to push for affirmative action in college admissions. She has been especially critical of the 10 percent plans instituted by universities in Texas as a substitute for affirmative action policies in admission decisions. "Simply guaranteeing admission to a certain percentage of students is not enough," Berry says. "The plans must be supplemented with proactive recruitment, financial aid, outreach, and academic support programs."[28] In promoting the policy in both employment and colleges, Berry remains one of the most influential proponents of affirmative action. Though affirmative action has become more unpopular, Berry views it as "a worldwide struggle ... one way of trying to achieve justice and opportunity."[29]

Stanley Fish

English and legal scholar Stanley Fish has also been a leading figure in the efforts to maintain, and even expand, affirmative action. Fish wrote an influential article in the early 1990s that, while seemingly dated, remains one of the most forceful defenses of affirmative action. Arguing not only for the continuation of affirmative action but also for additional remedies, Fish argued, "The belated gift of 'fairness' in the form of a resolution no longer to discriminate against [African Americans] legally is hardly an adequate remedy for the deep disadvantages that the prior discrimination has produced. When the deck is stacked against you in more ways than you can even count, it is small consolation to hear that you are now free to enter the game and take your chances."[30]

Since the publication of that article, Stanley Fish has remained a central figure in the affirmative action debate, especially in how the policy affects American education. Most recently he has called for a change in the terms of the debate. Responding to the critics of affirmative action who cast the policy as reverse racism, Fish has responded: "Let's stop asking, 'Is it fair or is it reverse racism?' and start asking, 'Does it work and are there better ways of doing what needs to be done?' Merely asking these questions does not guarantee that affirmative action will be embraced, but it does guarantee that the shell game of the search for neutral principle will no longer stand between us and doing the right thing."[31] Whether the policy is the "right thing," however, is subject to considerable debate, as the following examination of the opponents' position will illustrate.

OPPONENTS OF AFFIRMATIVE ACTION

Critics of affirmative action base their position on four distinct arguments as well. Like the arguments of supporters, the position of opponents includes two arguments that are abstract and two that focus on the tangible effects on the policy. First, and most important, opponents argue, affirmative action harms people who are not guilty of the social wrong the policy is aimed to correct, discrimination. Most opponents agree that affirmative action was necessary in the 1960s and 1970s but maintain that its time has passed; in other words, in weighing the benefits of affirmative action for African Americans versus the negative effects of the policy on whites (not getting a job, or not being admitted to a university, because of affirmative action), the pendulum has swung toward harming whites more than the policy helps blacks. This argument illustrates the fundamental disagreement between the two sides over the current status of racial discrimination in the country.

Next, opponents argue, affirmative action is detrimental to the important American tradition of merit-based social and economic advancement. In placing the interests of one group above all others, they say, affirmative action rewards physical characteristics like skin color rather than skill. Moreover, critics of the policy focus on two effects that they say harm society. In virtually guaranteeing positions based on race, affirmative action diminishes incentive and hard work, not only for candidates who attain jobs or college slots because of affirmative action but also for those who work or study alongside them. They point to recent gains in black students earning admission to college and graduate programs as evidence that affirmative action is not necessary any longer; as these students matriculate into their chosen occupations, any perceived obstacle to the doors of being lawyers, doctors, or professors will become less popular.

Finally, opponents maintain, affirmative action has the harmful impact of stigmatizing beneficiaries as not being capable, worthy, or competent; this stirring of resentment, in turn, blocks further progress in dismantling the racism that affirmative action is designed to change. Because the policy has run past its point of effectiveness, critics say, it is now doing more to engender questions about the competency of minority job candidates and of minority college students. If anything is unfair, argue opponents, it is a legitimate, worthy student whose capacity for work is questioned because of skin color; ending affirmative action would be a nod to its effectiveness during the 1960s and 1970s, as well as a recognition that the policy is now causing more harm than good.

Shelby Steele

Perhaps the most vocal critic of affirmative action as a theory and social issue is noted author Shelby Steele, a research fellow at the Hoover Institution. An African American, Steele has emboldened opponents of affirmative action and raised the hackles of supporters of the policy with his pointed arguments. In one of the most important books on the subject, *The Content of Our Character* (1990), Steele emphasized the negative impacts of affirmative action on African Americans. In particular, Steele argues, the policy has created a sense of victimization within black communities that paralyzes attempts to succeed at work or at school. In an interview regarding his position on the issue, Steele commented,

> My opposition to affirmative action has to do with my concern for black uplift. Affirmative action has created what I call a "culture of preference." It's not just a benign social policy having to do with college admissions. It is a vast and all-defining culture that continues to lock me in, as a black person, to a victim focused identity. Affirmative action makes me passive. It makes me into someone who cannot move forward unless white people are benevolent and help me move forward. It perpetuates dependency. I think affirmative action is the greatest negative force—the greatest force in opposition to black uplift—in society today.[32]

Summarizing succinctly the position of affirmative action's critics, Steele remains an influential figure in the debate.

Steele participated in dozens of public forums in the aftermath of the *Hopwood* and *Bollinger* decisions, staking out the position that affirmative action was a "fraud" and did little to change the inherent problems among African Americans that were the real culprits. In one particularly sharp editorial just two days after the *Bollinger* decision, Steele claimed that the decision was "a victory for white guilt" and would perpetuate the "anti-Americanism" of rewarding skin color instead of merit.[33] By emphasizing the view that building a color-blind, merit-based society produces more economic and educational uplift for African Americans, Shelby Steele provides an excellent example of the modern arguments against affirmative action.

Ward Connerly

The other major figure in the efforts to end affirmative action is Ward Connerly, the University of California regent who authored Proposition 209. Even several years after the Prop 209 controversy, Connerly remains a target for pro–affirmative action activists and a vocal spokesman for opponents of the policy. Like Shelby Steele, Connerly bases his opposition to affirmative action on the premise that the civil rights movement, among many things, laid the groundwork for a color-blind society. In a recent article, Connerly argued that the Civil Rights Act of 1964 "guaranteed that no person would be discriminated against in the public sphere, and that all Americans would be treated equally, 'without regard to race, color or national origin,' by the government. This perspective became known as the ideal of a 'color-blind society.'" Challenging the emphasis on diversity, Connerly concluded, "As America has changed into a more racially and ethnically diverse society, the color-blind ideal has begun to surrender to the perspective that we must 'celebrate our diversity.'"[34] Thus, as an important component of what many supporters and opponents contest is the very meaning of the 1960s civil rights movement, affirmative action has a social and political significance beyond its own importance as a public policy matter.

Connerly's recent authoring and campaigning for California Proposition 54—which would have limited the amount of ethnic and racial information that public institutions such as schools, hospitals, and governments could collect—highlighted his leadership in efforts to create a "race-blind" society. Though the proposition was defeated decisively, Connerly's plans to improve its language and resubmit it for consideration by voters in 2006 indicates that the debate over racial identity and affirmative action has not subsided.[35] Rather, in pitting competing interpretations of a basic, fundamental concept—the effectiveness, and even value, of a color-blind society—the debate over affirmative action is guaranteed to remain as one of the most controversial issues in American society for decades.

QUESTIONS AND ACTIVITIES

1. Organize your class into separate, small groups. Have each group create pro and con arguments for affirmative action. Debate the issue, using the arguments presented in the chapter.

2. In your small groups, prepare for another debate. Have each group adopt the perspective of different ethnic groups in the United States: African Americans, whites, Asian Americans, Native Americans, and Hispanics. What would each group think about the policy? How does your appreciation for each group's position change by role-playing as a member of that group?

3. In your final group activity, have each group adopt competing perspectives on Proposition 209. Debate its merits and weaknesses.

4. Create a timeline of the major events in affirmative action. Consider the following questions: Why are so many of the events court cases? What was the turning point in the origins of affirmative action? If you had to select one 5-year period that was the most important in affirmative action's history, what would it be? Why?

5. Consider the *Bakke* and *Bollinger* cases. Why has the Supreme Court sent such mixed signals over affirmative action?

6. In the *Bollinger* decision, Justice O'Connor predicted that affirmative action would no longer be necessary 25 years from now. Do you agree or disagree? Why?

7. Brainstorm all the possible ways that racism is evident in American society. Then brainstorm a list of possible solutions. Which have been, or are being, tried? Which have not been tried and should be? How does affirmative action fit within your own list of proposed solutions?

NOTES

1. President Lyndon B. Johnson's Commencement Address at Howard University, "To Fulfill These Rights," 4 June 1965, full text at Lyndon Baines Johnson Presidential Library and Museum Web site, http://www.lbjlib.utexas.edu/johnson/archives.hom/speeches.hom/650604.asp.

2. Andorra Bruno, "Affirmative Action in Employment: Background and Current Debate," Congressional Research Service, 1 December 1998.

3. Ibid.

4. Marquita Sykes, "The Origins of Affirmative Action," National Organization for Women Web site, http://www.now.org/nnt/08–95/affirmhs.html.

5. Bruno, "Affirmative Action in Employment."

6. Executive Order 11246: Equal Employment Opportunity, issued September 24, 1965, Federal Register, National Archives and Records Administration Web site, http://www.archives.gov/federal_register/codification/executive_order/11246.html.

7. See amended version of Executive Order 11246, http://www.archives.gov/federal_register/codification/executive_order/11246.html; Bruno, "Affirmative Action in Employment," 6.

8. *Regents of the Univ. of Cal. v. Bakke*, 438 U.S. 265 (1978).

9. Lincoln Caplan, Dorian Freidman, and Julian E. Barnes, "The Hopwood Effect Kicks In on Campus," *U.S. News & World Report*, 23 December 1996.

10. See full text of Proposition 209, California Secretary of State Web site, 1996, http://vote96.ss.ca.gov/Vote96/html/BP/209text.htm.

11. Edward W. Lempinen, Pamela Burdman, and *Chronicle* staff, "Measure to Cut Back Affirmative Action Wins," *San Francisco Chronicle,* 6 November 1996.

12. Reynolds Holding, "Supreme Court Lets 209 Stand," *San Francisco Chronicle,* 4 November 1997.

13. Pamela Burdman, "Boalt Student Group Works to Bring Back Affirmative Action," *San Francisco Chronicle,* 25 March 1998.

14. Katia Hetter, "Bid Preferences Halted," *San Francisco Chronicle,* 29 July 2004.

15. Henry J. Reske, "Law School Affirmative Action in Doubt," *American Bar Association Journal,* May 1996, 22.

16. Justin Ewers, "A Glimpse of Life without Affirmative Action," *U.S. News & World Report,* 31 March 2003.

17. Charles Lane, "Affirmative Action for Diversity Is Upheld," *Washington Post,* 24 June 2003.

18. Ibid.

19. *Grutter v. Bollinger,* 539 U.S. 306, 1996.

20. Lane, "Affirmative Action for Diversity."

21. Ibid, A01.

22. *Income, Poverty, and Health Insurance Coverage: 2003,* U.S. Census Bureau, issued 26 August 2004, http://www.census.gov/prod/2004pubs/p60–226.pdf.

23. Texas Higher Education Coordinating Board report, http://www.thecb.state.tx.us/reports/html/0016/c.htm.

24. Chart from "The Remarkable and Steady Progress of African Americans in Higher Education, 1960–2002," *Journal of Blacks in Higher Education* Web site, http://www.jbhe.com/latest/030404_blacks_collegeDegree.html.

25. U.S. Department of Education, "Paige Cites Progress in Black Education but Notes Achievement Gap Has Widened over Past Two Decades," 14 October 2003, http://usinfo.state.gov/usa/blackhis/pr101403.htm.

26. Barbara Bergmann, *In Defense of Affirmative Action* (New York: Basic Books, 1996), 53–59, 33.

27. Tim Grant, "Affirmative Action Sends Beacon of Hope, Civil Rights Chief Says," *St. Petersburg Times,* 7 November 1995.

28. Charles Dervarics, "Civil Rights Commission Finds Fault with Percentage Plans," *Black Issues in Higher Education,* 2 January 2003, 6.

29. Harold McNeil, "Rights Advocate Sees Nation at a Crossroad," *Buffalo News,* 18 November 2000.

30. Stanley Fish, "Reverse Racism or How the Pot Got to Call the Kettle Black," *Atlantic Monthly* 272 (November 1993), 130.

31. Stanley Fish, "When Principles Get in the Way," *New York Times,* 26 December 1996.

32. Peter Robinson, interview with Shelby Steele, published in *Hoover Digest* 2 (1996), http://www-hoover.stanford.edu/publications/selections/962/steele.html.

33. Shelby Steele, "A Victory for White Guilt," *Wall Street Journal,* 26 June 2003.

34. Ward Connerly, "We Are Multi-Racial—But We Should Be Color-Blind," *Daily Telegraph* (London), 2 October 2003.

35. Haya El Nasser, "Voters Shoot Down Proposition on Collecting Racial Information," *USA Today,* 9 October 2003.

SUGGESTED READING

Bergmann, Barbara. *In Defense of Affirmative Action.* New York: Basic Books, 1996.

Berry, Mary Frances. *Black Resistance, White Law: A History of Constitutional Racism in America.* New York: A. Lane, Penguin Press, 1994.

Burdman, Pamela. "Boalt Student Group Works to Bring Back Affirmative Action." *San Francisco Chronicle,* 25 March 1998.

Caplan, Lincoln, Dorian Freidman, and Julian E. Barnes. "The Hopwood Effect Kicks In on Campus." *U.S. News & World Report,* 23 December 1996.

Connerly, Ward. "We Are Multi-Racial—But We Should be Color-Blind." *Daily Telegraph* (London), 2 October 2003.

Curry, George E., and Cornel West. *The Affirmative Action Debate.* New York: Addison, 1996.

Dervarics, Charles. "Civil Rights Commission Finds Fault with Percentage Plans." *Black Issues in Higher Education,* 2 January 2003.

Eastland, Terry. *Ending Affirmative Action: The Case for Colorblind Justice.* New York: Basic Books, 1997.

El Nasser, Haya. "Voters Shoot Down Proposition on Collecting Racial Information." *USA Today,* 9 October 2003.

Executive Order 11246: Equal Employment Opportunity, issued September 24, 1965. *Federal Register,* National Archives and Records Administration Web site, http://www.archives.gov/federal_register/codification/executive_order/11246.html.

Ewers, Justin. "A Glimpse of Life without Affirmative Action." *U.S. News & World Report,* 31 March 2003.

Grant, Tim. "Affirmative Action Sends Beacon of Hope, Civil Rights Chief Says." *St. Petersburg Times,* 7 November 1995.

Gratz v. Bollinger, 23 June 2003, U.S. Supreme Court Web site, http://a257.g.akamaitech.net/7/257/2422/23jun20031600/www.supremecourtus.gov/opinions/02pdf/02–516.pdf.

Grutter v. Bollinger, 23 June 2003, U.S. Supreme Court Web site, http://a257.g.akamaitech.net/7/257/2422/23jun20030800/www.supremecourtus.gov/opinions/02pdf/02–241.pdf.

Fish, Stanley. "Reverse Racism or How the Pot Got to Call the Kettle Black." *Atlantic Monthly,* November 1993.

———. "When Principles Get in the Way." *New York Times,* 26 December 1996.

Hetter, Katia. "Bid Preferences Halted." *San Francisco Chronicle,* 29 July 2004.

Holding, Reynolds. "Supreme Court Lets 209 Stand." *San Francisco Chronicle,* 4 November 1997.

Johnson, Lyndon B. "To Fulfill These Rights." Commencement address at Howard University, 4 June 1965. Full text at Lyndon Baines Johnson Presidential Library and Museum Web site, http://www.lbjlib.utexas.edu/johnson/archives.hom/speeches.hom/650604.asp.

Lane, Charles. "Affirmative Action for Diversity Is Upheld." *Washington Post,* 24 June 2003.

Lempinen, Edward W., Pamela Burdman, and *Chronicle* staff. "Measure to Cut Back Affirmative Action Wins." *San Francisco Chronicle,* 6 November 1996.

McNeil, Harold. "Rights Advocate Sees Nation at a Crossroad." *Buffalo News,* 18 November 2000.

Proposition 209, 1996. California Secretary of State Web site, http://vote96.ss.ca. gov/Vote96/html/BP/209text.htm.

"The Remarkable and Steady Progress of African Americans in Higher Education, 1960–2002." *Journal of Blacks in Higher Education* Web site, http://www. jbhe.com/latest/030404_blacks_collegeDegree.html.

Reske, Henry J. "Law School Affirmative Action in Doubt." *American Bar Association Journal,* May 1996.

Robinson, Peter. Interview with Shelby Steele, published in *Hoover Digest* 2 (1996), http://www-hoover.stanford.edu/publications/selections/962/ steele.html.

Skrentny, John David. *The Ironies of Affirmative Action: Politics, Culture, and Justice in America.* Chicago: University of Chicago Press, 1996.

Steele, Shelby. *The Content of Our Character: A New Vision of Race in America.* New York: St. Martin's Press, 1990.

———. "A Victory for White Guilt." *Wall Street Journal,* 26 June 2003.

Texas Higher Education Coordinating Board report, http://www.thecb.state.tx.us/ reports/html/0016/c.htm.

U.S. Census Bureau. *Income, Poverty, and Health Insurance Coverage: 2003.* Issued 26 August 2004, http://www.census.gov/prod/2004pubs/p60–226.pdf.

U.S. Department of Education. "Paige Cites Progress in Black Education but Notes Achievement Gap Has Widened over Past Two Decades." 14 October 2003. http://usinfo.state.gov/usa/blackhis/pr101403.htm.

Videos

Major, Mary. *Story of a People, Volume 4: Affirmative Action on Trial.* Xenon Entertainment, 1998.

Woodruff, Judy, Lary Lewman, Thomas Lennon, and Thomas Bagwell. *Racism 101.* Alexandria, Va.: PBS Video [distributor], 1988.

Web Sites

Affirmative Action Timeline, http://www.factmonster.com/spot/affirmativetimeline1. html.

Debating Racial Preference Web site, http://www.debatingracialpreference.org/.

Issues in Depth: Affirmative Action, *Chronicle of Higher Education* Web site, 2004, http://chronicle.com/indepth/affirm/affirm.htm.

5

EDUCATION: SCHOOL CHOICE

"Today begins a new era," President George W. Bush remarked in January 2002, "a new time for public education in our country. Our schools will have higher expectations—we believe every child can learn. From this day forward, all students will have a better chance to learn, to excel, and to live out their dreams."[1] Signing the landmark No Child Left Behind Act, President Bush succeeded in updating federal policy on education for the first time since 1965. With the black-white achievement gap—the difference in dropout rates and academic skills—between white and black students persisting, one central component of No Child Left Behind was designed to bring the performance of African American students up to the national average. To do so, the bill's authors and the president included the first attempt to institutionalize school choice—in particular, vouchers and charter schools—at the national level. Today, with more than 40 percent of the nation's school districts offering some form of school choice, education policy has come to focus on the effectiveness of these reforms to the traditional public school model.[2]

Vouchers, which are tuition credits provided by local, state, or federal government, allow public school students to attend a school of their choosing. In some states, the choice is to attend another public school; in others, students may elect to use their voucher to offset the costs of attending a private school. Charter schools take school choice one step farther: they are built as a separate entity from public schools, even though local school boards or state education agencies sponsor them. Often dedicated to a particular field, such as the humanities or the sciences, charter schools have become an increasingly popular segment of the American public education system. With only one-half of the nation's African American students graduating from high school, black students constitute the core target for both voucher and charter school proposals. Consequently, school choice is one of the central contemporary issues facing African Americans. This chapter explores the most significant arguments of supporters and opponents of school choice.

HISTORICAL CONTEXT

The concept of school vouchers is almost as old as American public education itself. In fact, even before the first American advocates for public schools became active on the issue, political theorists argued that vouchers would use the free market as a tool for educating the masses. Adam Smith, one of the founding thinkers of modern libertarianism and conservatism, was the first to conceptualize vouchers. In 1778, Smith suggested that states should provide parents with tuition money for their students to attend school. Because there were no public schools at that time, the debate over using such an idea was a matter of governments even spending money for education, as opposed to the current form of the debate, which focuses on which system—government-run schools or government-funded school choice—was more effective. By the end of the eighteenth century, Thomas Paine, whose pamphlet *Common Sense* helped to ignite the American Revolution 20 years earlier, argued that state governments should provide tuition money for poor families. Thus, both the public education and voucher movements were born.[3]

During the early nineteenth century, the first public school systems were established. Led by Massachusetts, which in 1820 opened the nation's first public high school, states formed what was then known as common schools. These tended to be large, single-room buildings where students of all ages learned together. In the South, where most of the nation's African American population lived as slaves, the rudimentary education systems created were not open to black students. Much more controversial during the nineteenth century was the issue of keeping government funds out of private schools. Wary of using public money for tuition at religious schools, each state that developed a public school system decided against Adam Smith's ideas of vouchers. This sensibility of delineating public funds and religious institutions, which is very much ingrained in American politics, became even more pronounced at midcentury. In 1840, New York's Public School Society rejected Bishop John Hughes's request for state aid for Catholic students; two years later, New York's legislature passed the Maclay

Bill, which prohibited religious instruction in public schools. Nearly every state followed suit. Consequently, for nearly a century, the voucher debate became a minor issue in American education.[4]

That changed in the 1950s, a result of a renewed effort by conservatives to promote vouchers, and of the monumental *Brown vs. Board of Education* decision in 1954. That decision, which mandated desegregation in American schools, triggered a tremendous amount of academic research and subsequent political debate over the most effective method for instructing African American students. In addition to the *Brown* case providing the legal context for vouchers once again becoming a viable public policy, the idea of vouchers enjoyed renewed popularity during the 1950s. In particular, conservative economist Milton Friedman wrote an essay in which he revived the long-stagnant concept of vouchers and even coined the term voucher.[5]

The first voucher systems were established in 1957. Instead of being focused on educational effectiveness as the modern voucher and charter schools systems are, the voucher programs of the 1950s were a reaction by whites against the desegregation of the public schools. The so-called white flight academies were, at least officially, private schools, but the availability of state funds for tuition at these schools followed the concept of vouchers. Nonetheless, the corruption of the voucher idea, especially for segregationist ends, eventually did not withstand judicial muster. By 1970, the short-lived but once-thriving white flight academies of the South had been closed.

In the place of those academies came voucher and charter-school programs that met the spirit of the idea—school reform. Along with the monumental civil rights legislation of the 1960s, Congress passed the Elementary and Secondary Education Act (ESEA) of 1965. ESEA required the federal and state governments to dedicate additional resources toward improving education for economically disadvantaged students; because a disproportionate number of such students were African Americans, ESEA was the first step in restructuring the teaching and learning of black children. Furthermore, at the same time that ESEA was being developed, the Office of Economic Opportunity had developed a plan for a publicly funded voucher program experiment. In 1969, the Nixon administration further developed this concept and decided to implement the program in the school district of Alum Rock, California. Using federal money, the experiment was set up to last five years. But after disappointing results on standardized tests, the voucher program was deemed a failure, and the experiment ended in 1973.[6]

During the early 1970s, President Richard Nixon expanded the concept of vouchers with his idea of parochiad, whereby government monies could be used to offset the expenses of private schools. But before this quasi-voucher program could get under way, the U.S. Supreme Court blocked the practice.

In 1971, a majority of the justices decided in *Lemon v. Kurtsman* that the principle of separation of church and state forbade the mingling of public funds and private schools. Consequently, the first serious attempt to institutionalize vouchers on a nationwide scale died.[7]

Between the *Lemon* decision and 2001, voucher efforts were all focused on the state and local levels. As it had done in the nineteenth century, the state of New York took the lead on education reform in the 1970s. In 1971, the state legislature established a tuition grant program for low-income parents to use in private and religious schools. But, like President Nixon's parochiad system, the New York model was also struck down by the U.S. Supreme Court. In 1973, in *Committee for Public Education v. Nyquist,* the Court upheld its earlier ruling that public funds could not be used to finance private, religious schools. More than 30 years later, the *Nyquist* decision remains the last major hurdle for contemporary school choice proponents in their efforts to establish a national system of vouchers.[8]

But not just the Supreme Court opposed vouchers. Several times between 1970 and 1978, voters in Maryland and Michigan rejected ballot initiatives to create statewide voucher systems. Like the Court, the majority of the public was leery of mixing public monies with private, especially religious, schools. Moreover, fearful of a reduced commitment by federal and state government to public education, the time for vouchers had not yet come. That sentiment was confirmed throughout the 1980s as well, when President Ronald Reagan failed repeatedly to push through Congress a nationwide voucher system.[9]

That failure at the national level reinvigorated state-level efforts. In the late 1980s, as a bevy of studies indicated the abysmal state of public education in many American locales, advocates of vouchers and charter schools began pushing for pilot programs in the nation's most poorly performing school districts. In that strategy, advocates found success, as repeated efforts to improve education in American inner cities had failed. With an increasing sense by many Americans that any new idea was worth a try, the momentum for vouchers began to grow.

The first fruit of this new movement targeting inner cities came in Milwaukee, Wisconsin. In 1990, the Wisconsin legislature created the nation's first publicly funded voucher program. As discussed later in this chapter, the Milwaukee system became a model for other cities and states. Though voucher initiatives in California, Colorado, and Washington failed in the early and mid-1990s, proponents of vouchers and charter schools did score two major victories. In 1994, President Bill Clinton pushed through Congress a reauthorization of the Elementary and Secondary Education Act; one provision of the legislation was to provide seed money for charter school initiatives.[10] In addition, in 1995, citing Cleveland's deteriorating public school system, members of the Ohio state legislature created a city-wide voucher system for low-income families. Much like Milwaukee's, that system came into national focus because of seemingly endless court battles.

By the late 1990s, even with the Cleveland program in limbo because of legal challenges, proponents of vouchers enjoyed rising momentum nationwide. Significant defeats still occurred, most notably in Michigan and California. But in those locales where voucher proponents targeted low-income families in inner-city areas, and where the distinction between public funds and private schools was made clear, many parents embraced the idea. Their efforts culminated in the Florida legislature creating two voucher programs, one for disabled students and another for students in failing schools. By the early twenty-first century, vouchers and charter schools were entering the mainstream of American education. Whether that expansion continues is subject to intense debate.

No Child Left Behind Act

The bipartisan effort to overhaul the nation's 94,000 public schools was the culmination of many years of frustration with American education. In particular, desire to improve the plight of low-income students, especially African Americans and Hispanics, formed much of the motivation for the effort to correct the system. By updating the landmark Elementary and Secondary Education Act of 1965, this controversial legislation breaks from the past largely because it sets a variety of benchmarks for student progress and relies upon annual testing to determine whether schools are meeting them. More specifically, No Child Left Behind requires states to bring all students up to a proficient level on standardized tests by the 2013–2014 school year. In the meantime, each state must raise the level of proficiency each year. Schools that fail to make adequate progress for two consecutive years will receive technical assistance from the district and must give parents the opportunity to send their children to other campuses that have not been deemed as failing. Schools will be required to offer supplemental educational services including private tutoring chosen by the students' parents after a third year of failure to make adequate progress. After four consecutive years, a district is required to implement corrective action at the school, including adopting a new curriculum or replacing staff members. After five consecutive years of inadequate progress, a school would be identified for reconstitution or change in governance structure.[11] These provisions are seen as stepping stones to a nationwide school choice system in the future.

Secretary of Education Rod Paige talks to reporters, April 2004, during a press conference before a forum discussing the No Child Left Behind Act, Rock Bridge High
School, Columbia, Missouri (AP Wide World Photo/L. G. Patterson).

Standardized tests (which chapter 6 examines) are central to the No Child
Left Behind Act. States must begin administering annual statewide assessments in reading and mathematics in grades 3–8 and at least once during
grades 10–12 by the 2005–2006 school year. The tests must be aligned with
state academic standards; allow student achievement to be comparable from
year to year; be of objective knowledge; be based on measurable, verifiable,
and widely accepted professional assessment standards; and not evaluate
family beliefs. Teachers hired with funds from Title I—the first section of
the 1965 legislation that focused on disadvantaged students—had to meet
that criteria by the end of the school year that ended in 2003. Many states
had been working on increasing the ranks of qualified teachers prior to the
passage of the law.[12]

Funding and the way federal monies flow to schools were altered in the No Child Left Behind law as well. The final bill authorized several hundred million dollars for states to develop and administer assessments or to carry out other activities related to ensuring accountability for results in the state's schools or improving the quality of the assessments. The law changed the way that Title I funds are distributed to benefit schools with large concentrations of poverty. Despite the fact that No Child Left Behind boosts federal spending in public schools significantly, educators and elected leaders across the political spectrum argue that the legislation provides far less funding than is needed to achieve the lofty results it mandates. In fact, several states have considered forgoing Title I resources to avoid the requirements of the No Child Left Behind Law.[13]

African Americans largely welcomed No Child Left Behind. Though some black parents and leaders expressed concerns over the standardized tests, the accountability component of the law provided many with hope that the future for their children's education would be brighter. But involving the federal government so much has been controversial and forms the central rub between those who support the law and those who do not. Not surprisingly, those same supporters and opponents of No Child Left Behind are divided on the issue of school choice.

The Milwaukee Model

One focus of that debate, especially in how it pertains to African American students, is Milwaukee, Wisconsin. During the late 1980s, increasingly concerned by the onset of big-city educational problems—namely, declining academic performance and budget pressures—Milwaukee residents began seeking ways to reform their city's failing school system. In 1990, spearheaded by state representative Annette Williams, the Wisconsin legislature created the nation's first publicly funded voucher program. The Milwaukee Parental Choice Program (MPCP), as a pilot program, was set to operate only in Milwaukee, and only for 1,000 low-income students (defined as at or below 175% of the national poverty rate). By providing tuition vouchers for any nonsectarian private school, the state tried to avoid the legal challenges to earlier voucher efforts that included religious schools.[14]

The first students received their vouchers and began attending their new schools in 1990. Three-quarters of the enrollees were African Americans. In spite of a lawsuit filed by the American Civil Liberties Union in late 1990, the program continued; ultimately, this initial challenge to the Milwaukee system was denied by the Wisconsin Supreme Court, which upheld its constitutionality. Even though an important fifth-year study of the program indicated "mixed results" and declared that "choice and public school students were not much different," the program was popular among parents of voucher recipients.[15] Nonetheless, with only a lukewarm endorsement by the politically important study, advocates of the Milwaukee program were once again busy fending off challenges to the system.

Equally important in the fifth year of the program was that the Wisconsin legislature expanded it to include religious schools. Motivated to broaden the eligible schools by the mixed results of the fifth-year study, legislators determined to take a risk in challenging the legal precedent against using publicly funded vouchers for religious schools. Shortly after the 1995 expansion of the program, the ACLU again filed suit, this time expecting an easy victory. The *Nyquist* case provided a clear precedent against precisely the kind of program that the Milwaukee system had become. For three years, while the case was pending, the participation of religious schools in MPCP was halted. Nonetheless, in 1998, the Wisconsin Supreme Court upheld the constitutionality of the program, having determined that its "secular purpose" did not violate the First Amendment.[16]

Having survived political and legal challenges, school choice supporters won a major victory over the MPCP. Since the 1998 expansion, enrollment has skyrocketed. From 341 students in seven schools during the 1990–1991 school year, the MPCP has grown to 13,268 students at 107 schools in 2003–2004.[17] Undoubtedly, more positive assessments of the program's effectiveness have impacted the spike in enrollment: a report released in September 2004 showed a significantly higher graduation rate at voucher schools (64%) than at public schools (36%). With African Americans constituting such a large majority of voucher school students, the popularity of the MPCP continues to grow among the city's black parents.[18]

But the program's apparent success has provoked new controversy. In late 2004, for the first time in the MPCP's history, enrollment is near the maximum of 14,800 students (15% of the Milwaukee Public School system's enrollment). For the enrollment cap to be increased, the state legislature would have to alter the existing formula. But opponents of school choice contend that because the voucher system is "unaccountable" to taxpayers, no more than the existing $87 million annual cost should be spent. Once again ground zero for the school choice debate, Milwaukee and its voucher program seem likely to remain important examples for both sides.[19]

The Cleveland Model

In the early 1990s, emboldened by the Milwaukee example, Ohio political leaders began laying the groundwork for a similar system in Cleveland.

In June 1995, the Ohio state legislature created the Cleveland Scholarship and Tutoring Program (CSTP). Originally designed for grades K–3, the program was set to expand by one grade each year through grade 8; subsequent legislation has expanded the program further, providing for the coverage of grade 12 by the 2006–2007 school year. Cleveland-area families whose incomes are below 200 percent of the national poverty line are eligible. As the first publicly financed voucher program to include religious schools— the 1995 expansion of the Milwaukee system came later—the CSTP became a quick target for opponents of school choice.

The first legal challenge to the Cleveland model came early. From 1995 to 1999, opponents claimed in state court that the program violated the Ohio state constitution's ban against church and state institutions merging operations. In 1999, the Ohio Supreme Court upheld the legality of the program. Then, just one day before classes were set to start in 1999, a federal judge halted the program on the grounds that it violated the religious establishment clause of the U.S. Constitution. His decision was quickly vacated, or temporarily reversed, by the U.S. Supreme Court until appeals had been exhausted. Finally, in June 2002, the U.S. Supreme Court determined the Cleveland program's fate.[20] In *Zelman v. Simmons-Harris,* the Court ruled that the program did not violate the Constitution. Justice Sandra Day O'Connor, part of the 5–4 majority, concluded:

> The Ohio program is neutral in all respects toward religion. It is part of a general and multifaceted undertaking by the State of Ohio to provide educational opportunities to the children of a failed school district.... The program permits the participation of *all* schools within the district, religious or nonreligious. Adjacent public schools also may participate and have a financial incentive to do so. Program benefits are available to participating families on neutral terms, with no reference to religion. The only preference stated anywhere in the program is a preference for low-income families, who receive greater assistance and are given priority for admission at participating schools.[21]

Though this was not the complete reversal of the *Nyquist* decision sought by voucher advocates, the *Zelman* decision sparked a renewed momentum for school choice supporters.

Finally able to operate unfettered from legal wrangling, the CSTP witnessed steady growth. From 1,994 enrollees in 1996–1997, the program grew to 5,098 students in 2003–2004.[22] African Americans constitute 60 percent of students enrolled in the program, which is similar to the proportion of black students in Cleveland public schools. Research on the effectiveness of the program has been inconclusive, which both supporters and opponents of school choice have tried to use to their advantage.

FRAMING THE ISSUE

School choice, especially as it pertains to African Americans, has provoked a vigorous debate. Most central to the debate is the question of which type of system—the traditional school model, voucher programs, or charter schools—is most effective at providing each American student with equal access to a good education. Unlike the debate on other issues covered in this book, both supporters and opponents of school choice have the same goal: improving American public education. That their divide on the public policy matter of school choice is so wide speaks volumes about the growing strength of the school choice movement, and about the fear many opponents have about the nation's education system deteriorating further if school choice is implemented further.

Supporters of school choice typically advance three major arguments. The first is that vouchers and charter schools are the only way to ensure the constitutionally mandated right to equal access to a good education. With no debate that many of the nation's schools—particularly those in inner cities where the African American population is high—have declined in quality since the mid-twentieth century, school choice supporters maintain that such schools no longer provide a proper education for the students who attend them. Second, supporters advance an economic efficiency argument. They claim that in spite of a tremendous amount of funding per pupil (as of 2004, the national average was $8,208), the quality of American public education continues to decline. Handing parents vouchers not only makes the receiving school more directly accountable for that money but also increases the feeling of ownership among students and parents. At charter schools, supporters argue, the spending per student actually goes much farther, as the bureaucratic red tape of the public schools can be averted to some extent. Finally, supporters charge that concerns over separation of church and state are outdated and, to some extent, misunderstood. They point to recent Supreme Court decisions as evidence that even the Court recognizes the folly of the 1973 *Nyquist* decision. An imminent reversal of that decision, supporters hope, would delete the final obstacle to implementing school choice nationwide.[23]

Opponents of school choice also advance three major arguments. Denying that school choice is the best method for achieving equal access to a quality education, opponents maintain that using public resources for vouchers and charter schools drains much-needed funds from public school systems. Rather than divert those monies to school choice programs, opponents argue that such funds would be better spent on higher teachers' salaries and repairing dilapidated school buildings. Second, choice opponents charge that vouchers and charter schools are unproven, making it that much more unacceptable that public funds would be diverted to them from traditional public schools. They point to a handful of cases—such as the first voucher experiment in Alum Rock, California, and early studies from Cleveland—as evidence that vouchers are not nearly as effective as their proponents suggest. Likewise, they use a larger body of research on charter schools that illustrates lagging test performance by students in those schools. Third, opponents of school choice express concern that vouchers may be a way to insert a religious agenda into the nation's public schools. With the Supreme Court seeming to warm to the idea of using vouchers in private religious schools, choice opponents suggest that vouchers are a back-door method of advancing the religious beliefs of some choice advocates.[24] Not surprisingly, this claim is controversial in and of itself. Taking a closer look at the arguments of each position, and at the most visible activists on each side, will provide a more detailed context for understanding the school choice debate.

SUPPORTERS OF SCHOOL CHOICE

Advocates of vouchers and charter schools run the political gamut from political conservatives disenchanted with what they call the public school monopoly to African American parents concerned about their children's access to a good-quality education. Thus, while the pro-voucher and pro–charter school coalition may fracture on other political issues, their diversity has formed an influential voice in the school choice debate. Chester Finn, who served as President Reagan's assistant secretary of education, recently argued, "The best argument for choice is to enable poor people to have the same rights and opportunities that rich people already have by virtue of being rich. They move to where they want to buy a house, because of the schools or they send their kid to a private school. It's poor people who typically get trapped in bad schools and can't afford to do anything about it."[25] In addition to advancing their three main arguments—the right to a high-quality education, the economic efficiency of school choice, and the exaggerated concern over using public funds for private school tuition—school choice supporters have begun using recent data to illustrate the academic achievement of students in voucher and charter schools. One observer has remarked that "the nation's 8 million Black students stand to benefit the most" from school choice, which would allow their parents to "bypass troubled neighborhood schools and explore alternative routes, sending their kids to magnet programs, single-sex academies or independently run charter schools; using tuition vouchers for private or religious schools; or educating children at home."[26] A closer examination of two of the most visible proponents,

Joseph Viteritti and the Black Alliance for Educational Options, will bring these arguments into sharper focus.

Joseph Viteritti

A public policy professor at New York University, Joseph Viteritti has become a major force in advocating reform. His 2002 book, *Choosing Equality: School Choice, the Constitution, and Civil Society,* has been used by local advocates of school choice to promote their cause.[27] Central to Viteritti's work on school choice is its positive effect on minority students, especially African Americans, whom Viteritti argues stand to benefit the most from the creation of a full-scale, nationwide system of vouchers and charter schools. Recent polls indicating overwhelming African American support for school choice indicate that most black families recognize that advantage. Viteritti argues, "The most compelling argument for school choice in America remains an egalitarian one: Education is such an essential public good for living life in a free and prosperous society that all people deserve equal access to its benefits."[28]

Viteritti completely rejects the notion of opponents that school choice programs divert resources from public schools and do so with little appreciable gain in student achievement. In a recent forum on school choice options, Viteritti explained this:

> In Cleveland ... each voucher recipient gets $2,250 in funding, compared to $7,746 appropriated to their public-school counterparts.... As a matter of principle this disparity is an inequitable and indefensible form of public policy that hurts disadvantaged children the most. It also puts into question ... evaluations that compare the performance of students in voucher programs with that of public school students. If the worst that can be said of these programs that operate under such adverse conditions is that their students do no better [than public school students], then one must wonder how much better the same students would do if they received adequate funding.[29]

By turning on its head one of the central arguments of opponents of school choice, Joseph Viteritti has expanded his influence as the single most important public policy advocate of vouchers and charter schools.

Black Alliance for Educational Options

As the most powerful coalition of African Americans supporting school choice, the Black Alliance for Educational Options (BAEO) has maintained significant political pressure on opponents of choice. The BAEO has been particularly focused on advocating vouchers and charter schools, as both options usually involve a higher proportion of African American students than students of other backgrounds. Consequently, leaders and members of the organization have been instrumental in extending school choice programs in cities such as Detroit and in providing political pressure in Florida and Colorado, where school choice has become a central public policy issue.

The BAEO does so by emphasizing what it sees as the distortions spread by opponents of school reform. Most notably, the organization has corrected the commonly spread myth that school choice programs are selective; instead, the group's leaders argue, each school choice program in existence today uses a need-based formula to determine eligibility for the program. Because this benefits a disproportionate number of African American families, the BAEO has grown in membership and political sway. "This is a civil rights issue, especially for parents of color," says Kaleem Caire, president of the BAEO. "Each parent, and not just the wealthy, deserves the right to send his or her children to the school that best meets their needs."[30]

OPPONENTS OF SCHOOL CHOICE

Opponents of vouchers and charter schools are equally vocal, and equally well organized. Comprised primarily of a coalition of teachers' unions and politically liberal policy makers, anti–school choice activists emphasize the draining of public resources from existing schools, the unproven results of these new schools, and the danger of mixing public funds with religiously affiliated schools.

School choice opponents question the effectiveness of diverting resources from public schools to unproven institutions. For example, a 2002 report in *Education Week* concluded, "Originally designed to inspire innovation and free schools from bureaucracy, in return for showing results, charter schools often remain mired in debate over what they should look like and how they should be regulated and financed."[31] School choice opponent Jonathan Kozol, who wrote an indictment of the voucher movement in his book *Savage Inequalities,* went even further. He argues that school choice advocates are "proposing a voucher of a couple thousand dollars which at best would allow a handful of poor children or children of color to go to a pedagogically marginal private school."[32]

Congressman Harold Ford Jr., a Democrat from Tennessee, focuses on the limited impact vouchers might have on improving education, even if one accepts that they have the effects their supporters suggest they have. "Let's assume for a moment that we switch to a voucher system and give every parent a $3,000 or $4,000 voucher," Ford says. "How do you [stop schools from] raising their tuitions and pricing out many of the families we want to help the most?" According to Ford, the beneficiaries of such a system are not students at underperforming schools, as vouchers proponents maintain, but middle- and upper-income families who could afford the increased tuition at those private schools.[33]

Another problem is funding. Representative Ford has been equally vocal on this matter. Proponents of vouchers, Ford argues, focus on "5% or 10% of the children who are presently in the public school system, leaving the other 90% or 95% of the kids in the system at a further disadvantage." As a result, there simply is not enough money to finance vouchers for every public school student who wants to attend a private school.[34]

Moreover, school choice opponents maintain, that diversion of resources often goes to religious schools. The National Education Association, while offering a lukewarm endorsement of charter schools, adamantly opposes vouchers on those grounds. "Despite desperate efforts to make the voucher debate about 'school choice' and improving opportunities for low-income students, vouchers remain an elitist strategy," the organization declares. "Privatization strategies are about subsidizing tuition for students in private schools, not expanding opportunities for low-income children."[35] Calling into question the very motivation of school choice supporters, opponents have developed a politically potent case against the pro-school choice tide.

People for the American Way

A particularly influential organization in the school choice debate, People for the American Way has funded dozens of campaigns against ballot initiatives proposing vouchers. The organization bases its opposition on three criticisms of vouchers: the diversion of resources from public schools, the unproven effectiveness of voucher programs, and the alleged influence of religious groups in publicly financed voucher programs.

The diversion of resources from public schools is perhaps the most politically potent argument that People for the American Way (PFAW) has used in its various advertising campaigns. Those efforts often cite the example of Milwaukee's Student Achievement Guarantee in Education (SAGE) program, which was designed to decrease class sizes, improve curriculum, and promote parental involvement. According to PFAW, in spite of SAGE's popularity, and in spite of early studies pointing to its effectiveness, budget constraints resulted in a tightening of the program's finances. Most problematic, argues the organization, is that SAGE was cut by precisely the same amount that Milwaukee's voucher system grew. In the zero-sum arena of education dollars, PFAW maintains that vouchers are drains on the already pinched public education system.[36]

This diversion is made worse, the group argues, because vouchers have not been proven to be effective. Though each side can cite evidence that seemingly confirms its position, PFAW cites a 2002 U.S. Government Accounting Office report that shows no significant achievement gain for students under such programs (the same study does, however, show such a gain for African American students). Furthermore, the group maintains, results from Milwaukee and Cleveland do not demonstrate appreciable differences in reading and math skills between voucher and public school students. Though the debate over effectiveness is rife with the selective use of statistics, at the very least, those studies cited by PFAW have caused many potential supporters to reconsider voucher and charter school proposals.[37]

PFAW also expresses concern over the use of public money in private schools. The organization, in fact, has been most vocal about this issue. It argues that voucher programs "threaten students' religious liberty.... the provision of public funds to [religious] schools forces taxpayers to subsidize religion. This forced subsidization of religion violates freedom of conscience and is, we believe, completely contrary to the intent of the Founders and the core principles behind the constitutional separation of church and state."[38] Through lobbying state legislators, filing legal briefs with courts, and financing ad campaigns against voucher initiatives, PFAW has become a major opponent to the efforts of school choice advocates.

Primarily a social justice group, PFAW has also created the African-American Ministers Leadership Council, which has worked to offset the increasing popularity of vouchers and charter schools among African Americans. Reverend Timothy McDonald, chair of the ministers' group, charges that the main reason behind vouchers is to subsidize private, Christian schools. Observing that many Christian schools "are running out of money," McDonald warns against using public funds to finance religiously affiliated schools.[39] In 2002, in testimony to Congress on the issue of school choice, McDonald suggested that "voucher programs rob the majority of African American public school students, and students in general, of precious resources."[40]

Obviously, both supporters and opponents of school choice have staked out well-defined positions. With school choice remaining very popular among African Americans, the issue will continue to be important not only for them but also for the nation as a whole. The comments of one observer ring especially true: "Whether choice benefits children as much as it can— or whether it does little to help those most in need—depends upon how we Americans decide to govern it."[41]

QUESTIONS AND ACTIVITIES

1. What are the differences between vouchers and charter schools? In what settings might vouchers be better than charter schools, and vice versa?

2. Organize your class into two sides: pro–school choice and anti–school choice. Imagine that you are state legislators debating a bill proposing vouchers. Why should you vote for or against the bill? What is the most convincing evidence that you can offer as support for your position? Do the arguments change if you debate a bill authorizing charter schools?

3. Now imagine that each member of your class is a member of Congress. Should you pass a bill that would establish a national system of vouchers and charter schools? What different issues exist in this debate as compared to a state- or local-level debate?

4. From your perspective as a student, discuss what each the following offers that the other options do not: public schools, private schools, vouchers, charter schools, homeschooling. Does your perspective change as a parent? A teacher? A principal?

5. Given the historical background of American public education and the current debate over school choice, what do you think American education will look like 10 years from now? In 25 years? In 50 years?

6. Research what school choice proposals are in effect and are being debated in your state. Prepare a report that summarizes both the positive and negative responses to the plans.

NOTES

1. Committee on Education and the Workforce, Press Release, "President Bush Signs Landmark Education Reforms Into Law," U.S. House of Representatives, 8 January 2002.

2. Mary Lord, "Freedom of Choice," *Essence,* August 2003.

3. Sarah Mondale, ed., *School: The Story of American Public Education* (Boston: Beacon Press, 2002), part 1.

4. Joel Spring, *The American School, 1642–2000* (New York: McGraw-Hill, 2000), chap. 5.

5. Milton Friedman, "The Role of Government in Education," in *Economics and the Public Interest,* ed. Robert A. Solo (Rutgers, N.J.: Rutgers University Press, 1955).

6. Spring, *American School.*

7. *Lemon v. Kurtzman,* 403 U.S. 602 (1971).

8. Barbara Miner, "Supreme Court Debates Vouchers," *Rethinking Schools Online,* Spring 2002, http://www.rethinkingschools.org/special_reports/voucher_report/vdeba.shtml.

9. "A Brief History of Vouchers," People for the American Way Web site, http://www.pfaw.org/pfaw/general/default.aspx?oid=11827.

10. "Clinton Signs Educaton Bill Into Law," *Jet,* 7 November 1994.

11. Provisions of the law are explained in depth at the No Child Left Behind Web site, which is maintained by the U.S. Department of Education. See http://www.nclb.gov.

12. No Child Left Behind Web site, http://www.nclb.gov.

13. Diana Jean Schemo, "New Chief to Face Growing Resistance to Law," *New York Times,* 16 November 2004.

14. "Milwaukee Parental Choice Program," School Choice Info Web site, http://www.schoolchoiceinfo.org/facts/index.cfm?fl_id=1.

15. John F. Witte, Troy D. Sterr, and Christopher A. Thorn, "Fifth-Year Report: Milwaukee Parental Choice Program," Department of Political Science and the Robert M. La Follette Institute of Public Affairs, University of Wisconsin–Madison, 1995, http://www.lafollette.wisc.edu/Publications/OtherPublications/Education/1995/MilwaukeeChoice5YR/fifthYear.html.

16. "A Brief History of Vouchers," People for the American Way, http://www.pfaw.org/pfaw/general/default.aspx?oid=11827.

17. "Milwaukee Parental Choice Program," School Choice Info Web site, http://www.schoolchoiceinfo.org/facts/index.cfm?fl_id=1.

18. Alan J. Borsuk, "Graduation Rates Under Choice Higher," *Milwaukee Journal Sentinel,* 29 September 2004.

19. Sarah Carr, "Voucher Debate Flares as Program Nears Its Limit," *Milwaukee Journal Sentinel,* 25 October 2004.

20. Joseph P. Viteritti, "Vouchers on Trial," *Education Next,* Summer 2002.

21. *Zelman v. Simmons-Harris,* 536 U.S. 639, 2002.

22. "Enrollment Growth: Cleveland Scholarship and Tutoring Program," School Choice Info Web site, http://www.schoolchoiceinfo.org/facts/index.cfm?fpt_id=5&fl_id=2.

23. Terry Moe, *Schools, Vouchers, and the American Public* (New York: Brookings Institution Press, 2002).

24. Edd Doerr, Albert J. Melendez, and John M. Swomley, *The Case Against Vouchers* (New York: Prometheus Books, 1996).

25. "Choosing or Losing: The School Choice Controversy," School: The Story of American Public Education Web site, 2001, http://www.pbs.org/kcet/publicschool/roots_in_history/choice.html.

26. Lord, "Freedom of Choice," 178.

27. Joseph P. Viteritti, *Choosing Equality: School Choice, the Constitution, and Civil Society* (New York: Brookings Institution Press, 1999).

28. Richard W. Garnett, "The Justice of School Choice," *Weekly Standard,* 13 December 1999.

29. Joseph P. Viteritti, "Empowering the Poor," *Boston Review,* October/November 2003, 52.

30. Tamara Henry, "Voucher Debate Spills Into the Street," *USA Today,* 21 February 2002.

31. Alan Richard, "States' Work on Charters Still Unfolding," *Education Week,* 20 March 2002. pp. 1, 18.

32. Quoted on "School: Choosing or Losing" Web site, http://www.pbs.org/kcet/publicschool/roots_in_history/choice.html. See also Jonathan Kozol, *Savage Inequalities: Children in America's Schools* (New York: HarperCollins, 1991).

33. Joyce Jones, "The Problems with Education Coupons," *Black Enterprise,* February 2001.

34. Ibid, 21.

35. "Vouchers," National Education Association Web site, http://www.nea.org/vouchers/.

36. "Facts about Vouchers: Diversion of Resources for Public Education," People for the American Way Web site, http://www.pfaw.org/pfaw/general/default.aspx?oid=5452.

37. "Quick Voucher Facts: Do Vouchers Work?" People for the American Way Web site, http://www.pfaw.org/pfaw/general/default.aspx?oid=7660.

38. "Facts About Vouchers: How Do Vouchers Affect Religious Liberty?" People for the American Way Web site, http://www.pfaw.org/pfaw/general/default.aspx?oid=6954.

39. Evan Thomas and Lynette Clemetson, "A New War Over Vouchers," *Newsweek,* 22 November 1999.

40. Testimony of Rev. Timothy McDonald to the Subcommittee on the Constitution, Committee on the Judiciary, U.S. House of Representatives, 17 September 2002, http://www.house.gov/judiciary/mcdonald091702.htm.

41. Paul T. Hill, ed., *Choice with Equity: An Assessment by the Koret Task Force on K-12 Education* (Stanford, Calif.: Hoover Institution), 13.

SUGGESTED READING

Berliner, David C., and Bruce J. Biddle. *The Manufactured Crisis: Myths, Fraud, and the Attack on America's Schools.* New York: Addison Wesley, 1996.

Borsuk, Alan J. "Graduation Rates under Choice Higher." *Milwaukee Journal Sentinel,* 29 September 2004.

Carr, Sarah. "Voucher Debate Flares as Program Nears Its Limit." *Milwaukee Journal Sentinel,* 25 October 2004.

Chubb, John, and Terry Moe. *Politics, Markets, and America's Schools.* New York: Brookings Institution Press, 1990.

Committee on Education and the Workforce. "President Bush Signs Landmark Education Reforms Into Law" (press release). U.S. House of Representatives, 8 January 2002.

Doerr, Edd, Albert J. Melendez, and John M. Swomley. *The Case Against Vouchers.* New York: Prometheus Books, 1996.

Friedman, Milton. "The Role of Government in Education." In *Economics and the Public Interest,* edited by Robert A. Solo. Rutgers, N.J.: Rutgers University Press, 1955.

Garnett, Richard W. "The Justice of School Choice." *Weekly Standard,* 13 December 1999.

Henry, Tamara. "Voucher Debate Spills into the Street." *USA Today,* 21 February 2002.

Hill, Paul T. *Choice with Equity: An Assessment by the Koret Task Force on K-12 Education.* Stanford, Calif.: Hoover Institution, 2002.

Jones, Joyce. "The Problems with Education Coupons." *Black Enterprise,* February 2001.

Kozol, Jonathan. *Savage Inequalities: Children in America's Schools.* New York: HarperCollins, 1991.

Lord, Mary. "Freedom of Choice." *Essence,* August 2003.

McDonald, Rev. Timothy. Testimony to the Subcommittee on the Constitution, Committee on the Judiciary, U.S. House of Representatives, 17 September 2002, http://www.house.gov/judiciary/mcdonald091702.htm.

Miner, Barbara. "Supreme Court Debates Vouchers." *Rethinking Schools Online* (Spring 2002), http://www.rethinkingschools.org/special_reports/voucher_report/vdeba.shtml.

Moe, Terry. *Schools, Vouchers, and the American Public.* New York: Brookings Institution Press, 2002.

Mondale, Sarah, ed. *School: The Story of American Public Education.* Boston: Beacon Press, 2002.

Richard, Alan. "States' Work on Charters Still Unfolding." *Education Week,* 20 March 2002.

Schemo, Diana Jean. "New Chief to Face Growing Resistance to Law." *New York Times,* 16 November 2004.

Spring, Joel. *The American School, 1642–2000.* New York: McGraw-Hill, 2000.

Thomas, Evan, and Lynette Clemetson. "A New War Over Vouchers." *Newsweek,* 22 November 1999.

Viteritti, Joseph P. *Choosing Equality: School Choice, the Constitution, and Civil Society.* New York: Brookings Institution Press, 1999.

———. "Vouchers on Trial." *Education Next* (Summer 2002), http://www.educationnext.org/20022/24.html.

Witte, John F., Troy D. Sterr, and Christopher A. Thorn. "Fifth-Year Report: Milwaukee Parental Choice Program." Department of Political Science and the Robert M. La Follette Institute of Public Affairs, University of Wisconsin–Madison, 1995, http://www.lafollette.wisc.edu/Publications/OtherPublications/Education/1995/MilwaukeeChoice5YR/fifthYear.html.

Videos

Charter Schools That Work. Corporation for Educational Radio and Television, 2000.

SCHOOL: The Story of American Public Education. Stone Lantern Films, Inc., KCET, Hollywood, Calif., 2001.

Web Sites

Black Alliance for Educational Options, http://www.baeo.org.

Center for Education Reform, http://www.edreform.org.

"Choosing or Losing: The School Choice Controversy," *Roots in History,* PBS, 2001, http://www.pbs.org/kcet/publicschool/roots_in_history/choice.html.

No Child Left Behind Web site, maintained by the U.S. Department of Education. See http://www.nclb.gov.

"Public Education," People for the American Way, http://www.pfaw.org/pfaw/general/default.aspx?oid=12.

School Choice Info Web site, http://www.schoolchoiceinfo.org.

"Vouchers," National Education Association Web site, http://www.nea.org/vouchers/.

6

EDUCATION: STANDARDIZED TESTS

1. A _____ is concerned not with whether a political program is liberal or conservative but with whether it will work.

(A) radical (B) utopian (C) pragmatist D) partisan (E) reactionary[1]

2. Which of the following is the solution set of the equation $x^2 = 3x + 10$?

(A) $\{-2, -5\}$

(B) $\{-2, 5\}$

(C) $\{-5, 3\}$

(D) $\{-3, 5\}$

(E) $\{3, 5\}$[2]

Each year, millions of American students consider questions like these. On college entrance exams and on state-commissioned content tests, students' verbal, math, and social science skills are gauged. As an important tool for the American idea of meritocracy—the belief that advancement is based on ability and achievement—standardized tests may very well be the least popular aspect of education and employment in the United States. Mention ACT or SAT to most Americans, and horror stories of test anxiety and college admission failures abound. Regardless of racial, ethnic, or socioeconomic background, these institutions of American educational life spur considerable dissatisfaction among students, parents, and job seekers alike. But for the nation's largest ethnic minorities—African Americans and Hispanics—standardized tests strike a particularly dissonant chord. A long history of test bias—defined, generally, as the writing of questions that draw on aspects of culture and society that are less likely to be known by black students—has placed the standardized test industry in the middle of a firestorm. In the midst of that maelstrom lie some fundamental arguments over the continued importance of standardized tests. This chapter examines that debate by exploring how supporters and opponents of standardized testing deal with the accusation that such exams are biased against African Americans.

The Achievement Gap

Standardized testing has become the dominant method by which American students are evaluated. Tests are required for college admission, often making the difference between acceptance or denial. Standardized testing does not start at the college level, however. In fact, these tests are often given to students throughout their lives in the educational system, starting in elementary school and continuing all the way through college. Every state has standardized exams that determine the aptitude of students and their eligibility to advance to the next grade level; together, these two measurements are used to grade the school as a whole, with significant consequences applied to schools

Nine-year-old girl at school in Newport News, Virginia, 2004 (AP Wide World Photo/Jason Hirschfeld).

that do not meet the minimum standards for student achievement. Since 2001, when the No Child Left Behind Act was passed by Congress, standardized tests, and in particular their potential bias against African Americans, have become central issues in the school reform debate.

Standardized tests are also widely criticized as culturally inappropriate for many groups. Test opponents argue that in some cultures parents routinely reward children for answering unsolicited questions about the world, and that these children therefore have an advantage on tests of academic achievement. Criticism of content focuses on the differing relevance of the content to people from different cultures. A common example is giving newly arrived immigrants an intelligence test that asks them to name past leaders of the country to which they have recently immigrated.

For African Americans—and, to a lesser extent, other ethnic minorities such as American Indians and Hispanics—the issue is clear and straightforward. Since the wide-scale adoption of the SAT and similar tests in the 1960s, black students have consistently scored lower than members of other ethnic groups. The so-called achievement gap between white and black test takers may well be the consequence of a host of factors. But opponents of tests argue that the continuing disparity in test scores is the result of cultural bias in the content of questions. Largely, if not completely unintentional, this bias affects the educational achievement of African American students from their first years in elementary schools, all the way through college, and even in some professions. Obviously, then, the achievement gap is a significant public policy issue facing African Americans and the nation as a whole.

One anti-testing group, the Applied Research Center, contends that standardized tests "aggravate racial inequality." Whether used to evaluate schools or determine college admissions, or as high school exit exams, standardized tests "result in disproportionate numbers of people of color dropping out of school or being denied diplomas." Moreover, the group contends, racism exists not only in the tests themselves. "The high-stakes systems of rewards and sanctions they are tied to ... have inherent racial biases that often merely measure the past academic opportunities (or lack thereof) rather than assessing intelligence or predicting future performance." As a result, several colleges, such as the University of California's campuses, have decided to reduce the SAT's weight in admissions decisions or to drop the SAT as a factor altogether.[3] Even as the College Board works to develop improved versions of the test, the pressure simply to remove the exam as a factor remains high. "Like the poll tests of yesteryear," one critic observes, "today's high-stakes tests in effect deny learning and life opportunities to students of color."[4]

Like many issues examined in this book, the question of bias in standardized testing is asked in the context of overwhelming statistical evidence.

The most important part of that research can be seen in tables 6.1 and 6.2. Table 6.1 illustrates the achievement gap on the nation's most-used college admissions exam, the Scholastic Aptitude Test (SAT). Table 6.2 illustrates that gap on the other major college admissions test, the American College Test (ACT). Asian Americans, on average, score the best on the SAT and are followed closely by whites. Hispanics and African Americans lag behind those two groups; in fact, African Americans score the lowest among the groups, with average scores approximately 20 percent lower than those of whites and Asian Americans. Finally, table 6.1 also illustrates another facet of the test-bias issue: female test takers of all groups fare noticeable worse than males of the same background. While that issue is extraneous to the discussion of test bias against African Americans, it nonetheless serves to strengthen the argument of test opponents.

Some test makers have attempted to develop culture-neutral tests of intelligence, but on the whole these attempts have not been successful. Conceptions of intelligence vary widely from culture to culture, and abstracting the few common elements, or what appear to be the few common elements, cannot be depended on to produce a reliable guide to intelligence.[5]

HISTORICAL CONTEXT

Standardized testing began in the United States during the early twentieth century. Its first form was the Intelligence Quotient (IQ) test. Though the first

Table 6.1   SAT Verbal and Mathematical Scores by Gender and Race/ Ethnicity, 2004

	Whites	Asian Americans	African Americans	Hispanics
Males				
SAT–Math	551	577	444	495
SAT–Verbal	537	533	443	484
Composite	1088	1110	887	979
Females				
SAT–Math	515	543	427	462
SAT–Verbal	534	531	448	478
Composite	1049	1074	875	940

** National Average is 508 on Verbal, 516 on Math, and 1026 Composite.

Source: Howard T. Everson and Roger E. Millsap, *Beyond Individual Differences: Exploring School Effects on SAT Scores*, College Board Research Report No. 2004–3, 2004.

IQ test was given in 1905, it was first administered on a large scale during the late 1910s, when the United States entered World War I. Robert Yerkes, a proponent of standardized testing for college admissions, convinced the U.S. Army to use the IQ exam as a method for selecting officers. In administering the test to more than two million soldiers, Yerkes was also able to further his own mission of validating the use of testing for other means, namely as university entrance exams. Though many people today see standardized tests as an objective method for selecting the best-qualified applicant for admissions or for a profession, the origin of standardized testing has dubious cultural roots. Robert Yerkes and most of his contemporaries supported testing as a means of ensuring college slots and officer positions to the most intelligent. Because these tests were administered well before desegregation, the typical result of testing was that those slots and positions went to white, upper-class men.[6]

This did not bother Yerkes, as he was a proponent of eugenics. Coined by social scientist Francis Galton, eugenics called for selective breeding to improve intelligence. Eugenicists pervaded American politics during the late nineteenth and early twentieth centuries and saw standardized testing as a way to shut out peoples of supposed lower intellect—such as African Americans, Italians, and Irish—from colleges and military command. Though the eugenics movement faded after the 1920s, its influence in the development of the first standardized exams naturally continues to impact the argument of tests' opponents.[7]

Standardized testing fell out of favor with the American public during the 1930s and 1940s, to some extent because of its affiliation with the eugenics movement. But by the late 1950s, testing—without its earlier racist baggage—came back into favor because of the Cold War. Most importantly, the Soviet Union's successful launch of the first spaceship, *Sputnik,* in 1957 provoked a

Table 6.2 ACT Test Scores by Race/Ethnicity, 2004

Ethnicity	*Composite Score*
African American	17.1
Mexican American	18.4
American Indian	18.8
Puerto Rican or Other Hispanic	18.8
Asian American	21.8
White	21.8
National Average	20.9

Source: ACT Assessment Web site, http://www.act.org/news/data/04/index.html.

feeling of crisis within the United States. Long perceiving themselves as morally and intellectually superior to the Soviets, Americans were stunned that they had fallen behind in the space race. The commonly accepted explanation for that debacle was the failure of American schools to teach math and science. Thus, in order to ensure that American students were learning the basics, states began to administer end-of-year tests that gauged students' aptitude in particular subjects. Likewise, college admissions tests such as the SAT, which had been used on a limited basis since the 1920s, became common features of the college admissions process.[8]

The explosion in the number of college students during the 1960s and 1970s simply reinforced this momentum in favor of standardized tests. A litany of elementary and secondary school tests were added to ensure consistent levels of aptitude throughout a student's education. Most common were the Iowa Test of Basic Skills (ITBS), developed by Riverside Publishing, a division of Houghton Mifflin; the California Achievement Test (CAT), developed by CTB/McGraw-Hill; and the Metropolitan Achievement Test, developed by Harcourt, Brace Inc. Though many opponents to testing attempted to block the wide-scale usage of these exams on the grounds that they were biased against ethnic minorities and females, the public concern over American educational quality offset those efforts.

That concern grew during the 1980s and early 1990s as a number of reports indicated the declining state of education in the United States. This prompted the back to basics movement, which, like the calls for reform following *Sputnik,* charged that American schools had gotten away from teaching the fundamentals of reading, math, science, and history. To improve the situation, most states developed content-area learning standards that would be tested not only by teachers but by the state at the end of the year. This movement toward accountability culminated in 2001 with the No Child Left Behind Act, which takes that testing one step further by instituting a national test for content. Naturally, opponents to testing on grounds of racial bias have more reason now to fight the onset of such a program.

The Golden Rule Lawsuit

The controversy over racial bias in standardized tests is not limited to scholastic aptitude or college entrance exams. It also involves licensure examinations for particular professions. Teachers, police officers, fire department employees, and many civil service positions require applicants to pass certification tests as a condition of being hired. Because those employment tests involve the same kind of question format, the opportunity for bias exists. This issue exploded into a national controversy in the 1980s.

The subject of the racial bias controversy was another profession with licensure exams, the insurance industry. In 1976, the Illinois Department of Insurance hired Educational Testing Service (ETS) to develop a licensure test for insurance agents. The exam would be mandatory, meaning that any insurance company operating in the state would have to ensure its agents' passing of the test. One of those businesses, the Golden Rule Insurance Company, sued the state, arguing that the licensure test was biased against African Americans. Five unsuccessful applicants, all of whom were black, joined the suit with Golden Rule.[9]

The suit set off a controversy that rocked the standardized test industry. The major test makers—ETS and the College Board—commissioned a series of research studies intended to prove the unbiased nature of the exam. But performance differences on the test between white and black test takers overwhelmed such research. In 1984, Golden Rule Insurance Company and the state insurance department reached a settlement out of court. The main provision of the settlement was that ETS would use a hierarchy of questions that would minimize, if not completely erase, any racial bias in the exam.[10]

That hierarchy emphasized questions on which black and white applicants fared similarly. Thus, ETS would rank in priority order those questions. The other questions—those for which the racial performance differential was noticeable—might be used, but only once the first pool had been exhausted. The subsequent Golden Rule policy has been the subject of considerable debate since the settlement. One critic of the policy, Paul W. Holland, has argued, "All that the Golden Rule procedure did was to choose . . . test items on which Black test takers performed on average somewhat *higher* than usual and, simultaneously, White test takers performed on average somewhat *lower* than usual." The result, Holland charges, is that "both of the specially constructed types of test were biased in a sense that is . . . entirely undetectable by those who only look at the words in the test booklet to assess the bias of a test."[11] In spite of the controversy, five states considered legislation that would have enacted the Golden Rule policy.

ETS succeeded in blunting the momentum in favor of the procedure, however. Their flurry of studies showed that if the Golden Rule policy was applied to other exams—most notably, college entrance tests—those exams became even less accurate in predicting how the test taker would fare in college. There was little opponents could do to debate this point, given the method used to construct tests. Essentially, each of these standardized exams—the SAT, the ACT, or the Illinois insurance exam—is assembled with pools of questions with varying difficulty. The questions that have the greatest predictive power, or accuracy in forecasting how a student may fare in college, are those that are moderately difficult. Those were precisely the questions on which black and white test takers performed most differently. In short, by throwing out those questions, standardized exams become almost invalid statistically, at least in their accuracy in predicting things like college grade point average.[12] Thus, since the onset of the Golden Rule provision, opponents of tests have mostly avoided proposals that would alter exams but rather have called for their eradication altogether.

Types of Possible Test Bias

A well-known researcher studying the black-white achievement gap, Christopher Jencks, has isolated several different categories of possible test bias. Though Jencks is not firmly positioned with either supporters or opponents of tests, his categories of bias have helped opponents identify specific ways that standardized testing may disadvantage African Americans. The first type of bias is labeling bias. This arises from the misnaming of tests, such as the Scholastic Aptitude Test. Though most people think that the SAT measures something innate, or something that one is born with, other factors—such as educational quality, home environment, socioeconomics—factor largely into the performance of students on a test. Rather than measuring one's genetically designed intelligence, exams such as the SAT and ACT are merely predictors of college success based on those environmental factors. As such, Jencks argues, they give the false impression that African Americans and other ethnic minorities are by nature inferior intellectually.[13]

The second type of test bias is the one that most people think of when the issue is raised. Known as content bias, this problem is created by questions that favor one group over another. For example, using reading comprehension questions that come from a book well-known among white families but less popular for cultural reasons among African Americans will consistently give white students a distinct advantage; similarly, if test makers were to adopt a series of reading comprehension questions on Kwanzaa, the reverse situation would occur. It is precisely this type of bias that was the central issue in the Golden Rule lawsuit. With a seemingly infinite number of possibilities for content bias, this particular issue is one on which test makers, policy researchers, and activists on both sides focus.[14]

Finally, Jencks has discussed at length the problem of prediction bias. Though test makers often prefer not to discuss this aspect of their exams, many tests, including the SAT, ACT, and Armed Forces Qualification Test (AFQT), are used to predict performance in college or in the military. The problem, as the Golden Rule case illustrated, is that adjusting for content bias dramatically weakens the predictive power of standardized tests. Jencks explains:

> If black undergraduates typically earned higher grades than whites with the same SAT scores, most people would probably conclude that the SAT was biased against blacks. Likewise, if black recruits performed better in most military jobs than whites with similar AFQT scores, most people would say that the AFQT was biased against blacks. But that is not what we find. White undergraduates usually earn higher grades than blacks with the same SAT scores, and white recruits perform slightly better in most jobs than blacks with the same AFQT scores. This does not mean that either the SAT or AFQT is biased against whites. It merely means that whites who compete with blacks tend to have other advantages besides high test scores.[15]

As Christopher Jencks demonstrates, environmental forces form a significant part of the bias issue. While supporters and opponents of standardized testing both agree on that point, they remain divided over the degree to which such factors affect performance. In short, the issue of environmental forces versus bias frames the debate over standardized tests.

FRAMING THE ISSUE

Supporters of standardized testing embrace the concept of meritocracy and argue that exams are the vehicle by which merit is determined. Though most supporters lament the relatively poor performance of African Americans and other ethnic minorities on exams, they point to a host of explanations other than racial bias in tests. Most commonly, they suggest that the relatively recent integration of American public schools has just begun to bring African Americans into the cultural mainstream. Slowly but steadily improving tests scores over that time period, test supporters argue, bear out this analysis. Furthermore, they say, even if some tests are not culturally neutral, that is not an appropriate goal for American education. Supporters scoff at some proposals to include in a single test different pools of questions on which members of particular ethnic groups score better; in addition to being methodologically questionable, such a practice serves to splinter American society. In short, supporters of standardized testing conclude that recent efforts to make tests fair eliminate the historical problems with such tests and make them viable methods of determining which people—regardless of background—should obtain college admission, advance a grade, or land a job.

Opponents argue that tests are biased in their content and are not reliable indicators of African Americans' intelligence, scholastic aptitude, or academic performance. They contend that standardized tests by definition assume that all students have the same backgrounds, will understand and interpret material the same way, and will be able to apply their understanding similarly. In a nation as diverse as the United States, opponents maintain, students' drastically different backgrounds produce divergent cultural experiences and ways of learning. In many ways these tests are culturally biased, and the people who make them do not take into account the extremely diverse population of students they are targeting. Because these tests do not give every student an equal chance of success, opponents conclude that they should not be given the power to determine whether one is admitted to college or becomes certified in a particular profession.

SUPPORTERS OF TESTS

The problem with American education, test supporters argue, is not tests but curriculum. William Schmidt, an active supporter of standardized tests, is highly critical of American education. Schmidt contends that the nation's schools try to cover a broad swath of knowledge rather than focus on specific, related topics from grade to grade; this has the effect of giving American students a knowledge base that is "a mile wide and an inch deep." In particular, Schmidt suggests that middle-school classrooms are "intellectual wastelands in math and science," observing that American curriculum developers treat "math and science as a laundry list of separate things." Indicting the school system, Schmidt argues, "We worry more about hormones and self-confidence than intellectual challenges."[16]

Pointing to problems inherent in American schools is a central analytical feature of the supporters' case. Because there is no way to refute the black-white achievement gap on tests, supporters of tests maintain that something other than bias in questions is to blame. They cite a host of factors that contribute to the lagging performance of African American students. Parent participation, teachers' salaries, physical state of school buildings, and even nutrition are often listed as contributing factors in the performance of black students on tests.[17]

Supporters of tests also maintain that performance disparities on standardized exams are the result not of racial or cultural bias, but of poor education and socioeconomic factors. Naturally, then, many test supporters are also supporters of education reform, such as charter schools and vouchers (the subject of chapter 5). Significant evidence seems to support their contention about socioeconomic factors being the most important determinant in test scores. Tables 6.3 and 6.4 illustrate the clear correlation between annual family income and test performance on the SAT and ACT, respectively.

Table 6.3   SAT Test Scores for College-Bound Seniors by Family Income, 2004

Family Income (per year)	Verbal	Math	Total
< $10,000	422	450	872
$10,000 – $20,000	440	457	887
$20,000 – $30,000	459	467	926
$30,000 – $40,000	478	482	960
$40,000 – $50,000	493	496	989
$50,000 – $60,000	501	504	1005
$60,000 – $70,000	507	510	1017
$70,000 – $80,000	515	518	1033
$80,000 – $100,000	527	530	1057
> $100,000	553	562	1115
National Average	508	518	1026

Source: 2004 College Bound Seniors, The College Board, 2004,
http://www.collegeboard.com/prod_downloads/about/
news_info/cbsenior/yr2004/2004_CBSNR_total_group.pdf.

Table 6.4   ACT Test Scores for College-Bound Seniors, by Family Income, 2004

Annual Family Income	Composite Score
< $18,000	18.0
$18,000 – $24,000	18.7
$24,000 – $30,000	19.4
$30,000 – $36,000	19.9
$36,000 – $42,000	20.4
$42,000 – $50,000	20.9
$50,000 – $60,000	21.3
$60,000 – $80,000	21.9
> $100,000	23.5
National Average	20.9

Source: 2004 National Score Report, ACT, 2004, http://
www.act.org/news/data/04/pdf/t11.pdf.

Table 6.5   ETS's 14 Factors in Classroom and Test Performance

Early Development	The School Environment	Home Learning Environment
• weight at birth	• rigor of the school curriculum	• reading to young children
• lead poisoning	• teacher preparation	• TV watching
• hunger and nutrition	• teacher experience and attendance	• parent availability and support
	• class size	• student mobility
	• availability of appropriate classroom technology	• parent participation
	• school safety	

Source: "ETS Report: Achievement Gap Will Not Close without Understanding School and Societal Factors," ETS Web site, 20 November 2003, http://www.ets.org/news/03111801.html.

Educational Testing Service

The pioneer of standardized testing in the United States, ETS has a vested interest in maintaining the integrity of its examinations. While ETS has always had a large research budget to ensure the cultural fairness of its tests, it is also active in refuting the claims of opponents to standardized testing. The organization maintains a well-funded research arm that conducts dozens of studies each year; not surprisingly, much of that research focuses on the achievement gap between white and minority test takers.

Like other supporters of standardized testing, ETS sees the achievement gap as its single biggest problem. To defend its tests, as well as to propose reforms to the education system, ETS commissioned a major study in 2004. In *Parsing the Achievement Gap: Baselines for Tracking Progress,* the organization's researchers isolated 14 variables that affected classroom and test performance. Grouped into three major categories—early development, school environment, and home learning environment—these factors represent all of the reasons other than test bias that supporters say cause the achievement gap.[18] Table 6.5 illustrates those factors.

Thus, as charges mount that their exams are biased, ETS has emphasized a single argument: that just because group differences exist in test performance, that does not mean the test is flawed, or that it is biased. Other factors—such as family background, quality of school, quality of teachers in a particular subject—may be to blame. In a recent report for ETS, researcher Michael Zieky argues, "Group differences in performance are an important sign that there may be fairness problems with a test, but the differences alone are not proof that a test is unfair."[19]

OPPONENTS OF TESTS

Opponents of standardized tests counter the statistical evidence by pointing out that African Americans score even lower than the lowest socioeconomic category. This fact, opponents argue, indicates that while economic factors may indeed play an important role in test performance, additional factors—such as test bias—reduce African Americans' scores even further. When coupled with environmental factors, the most important of which may be the high number of black students in failing school districts, opponents argue that the centrality of standardized tests in grade promotion, college admissions, and professional certification seems patently unfair. One critic, V. E. Lee, contends, "Children's learning is strongly influenced by the contexts in which it occurs. Those contexts may be defined by the children's families, the classmates with whom they experience schooling, the peers with whom they choose to interact, and the teachers who instruct them." In short, Lee concludes, "Students are profoundly influenced by the schools they attend."[20] Without increased funding for majority-black schools and school districts, opponents maintain, African Americans' performance on standardized tests will not improve.

FairTest: The National Center for Fair & Open Testing

The most influential organization opposed to standardized testing is the National Center for Fair & Open Testing, better known as FairTest. The organization is dedicated to "eliminating the racial, class, gender, and cultural barriers to equal opportunity posed by standardized tests, and preventing their damage to the quality of education."[21] To achieve that goal, FairTest has lobbied Congress and several state legislatures to eliminate the use of high-stakes testing, mainly on the grounds that it is racially and culturally discriminatory.

FairTest has been particularly focused on a controversial requirement to play Division I college athletics, Proposition 16, which governs the initial eligibility requirements for student-athletes at more than 300 Division I colleges and universities of the National Collegiate Athletic Association (NCAA). Implemented in 1995, Proposition 16 precludes high school graduates who do not meet its standards from participating in intercollegiate competition. To qualify for full eligibility, student-athletes must have a 2.0 grade point average in 13 approved academic core courses and an SAT of 1010 or a combined ACT of 86. Students with lower test scores need higher core course GPAs. The minimum test score for students with a GPA of 2.5 or higher is 820 on the SAT and 68 on the ACT. FairTest argues that in addition to the cultural bias of the SAT and ACT, which disadvantages African American students, the disproportionately high number of black athletes in colleges results in a startling number of them being ruled ineligible for competition. Using NCAA research, the organization concludes that the test score requirement alone disqualifies African American student-athletes at 10 times the rate for white students.[22] As an example of the effects of test bias that many Americans can see clearly, FairTest has succeeded in increasing the pressure against test and policy makers.

In conclusion, there seems little middle ground on the issue of standardized tests. Supporters see recent steps by ETS, the College Board, and ACT as sufficient to address any questions of racial and cultural bias. As such, in the minds of supporters, standardized testing remains a crucial aspect of secondary and higher education as well as the certification process for teachers, insurance agents, doctors, lawyers, and a host of other professions. Opponents, on the other hand, see racial bias in standardized tests as merely one more example of institutionalized racism at all levels of American education. Undoubtedly, the enactment of the No Child Left Behind Act has increased, rather than quieted, concern over possible bias in exams. As certain features of NCLB take effect in the next few years—in particular, the assessment of certain schools as failures if their students' test scores are too low—the debate over racial bias in standardized tests will grow even more vocal.

QUESTIONS AND ACTIVITIES

1. Organize your class into two groups. One group should list the major arguments in favor of standardized testing; the other should list the major arguments against it. Debate the issue in class. Which arguments are the most persuasive?

2. Construct a timeline of the major events in standardized testing's history. With which national events do those events coincide?

3. What standardized tests do you have to take at your school? Can you think of any questions that might be construed as biased?

4. Research the testing requirements for K–12 in various states. Report to your class what you found. What seems to be the best system? The worst? Why or why not?

5. Imagine that opponents of tests get their way and that all standardized tests are banned. What does that change? How would college admissions be different? Certification for professions?

6. Are there alternatives to standardized tests, for both education and professional certification?

7. Identify some colleges or universities that do not require SATs. Report on why they don't require them and discuss the student makeup and student success there.

NOTES

1. Sample question from the 1999 SAT, *Frontline: Secrets of the SAT Web site,* http://www.pbs.org/wgbh/pages/frontline/shows/sats/where/1999.html.

2. Sample question for the New SAT, *Princeton Review Web site,* 2004, http://www.princetonreview.com/college/testprep/testprep.asp?TPRPAGE=553&TYPE=NEW-SAT-LEARN.

3. "Get SMART: Standards for Excellence and Equity in Public Education," Applied Research Center Web site, http://www.arc.org/erase/smart.html.

4. "Racial Profiling and Punishment in U.S. Public Schools," Applied Research Center Web site, 30 October 2001, http://www.arc.org/erase/profiling_summ.html.

5. Ken Richardson, *The Making of Intelligence* (New York: Columbia University Press, 2000), 17–18, 163–64.

6. Nicholas Lemann, *The Big Test: The Secret History of the American Meritocracy* (New York: Farrar, Straus and Giroux, 1999), 23–25.

7. Ibid., 23–25.

8. Ibid., 84–86.

9. Rebecca Zwick, *Fair Game? The Use of Standardized Admissions Tests in Higher Education* (New York: RoutledgeFalmer, 2002), 125–27.

10. "Test Service Accepts Safeguards against Bias," *New York Times,* 29 November 1984.

11. Paul W. Holland, "Causation and Race," Educational Testing Service Research Report #RR-03–03 (January 2003), 14, http://www.ets.org/research/dload/RR-03–03.pdf.

12. Zwick, *Fair Game,* 125–27.

13. Christopher Jencks, "Racial Bias in Testing," in *The Black-White Test Score Gap,* ed. Christopher Jencks and Meredith Phillips (Washington, D.C.: Brookings Institution, 1998), 55–86.

14. Ibid., 56.

15. Ibid., 57.

16. Mindy Cameron, "If We Set the Bar High, Our Children Will Compete," *Seattle Times,* 2 November 1997.

17. "Variables Play Role in Races' Achievement Gap," *Atlanta Journal Constitution,* 2 September 2004.

18. Paul Barton, *Parsing the Achievement Gap: Baselines for Tracking Progress* (Princeton, N.J.: Educational Testing Service, 2003). Available on the ETS Web site, http://www.ets.org/research/pic/parsing.pdf.

19. Michael Zieky, "Ensuring Fairness in Licensing Exams," Educational Testing Service Web site, Winter 2002, http://www.ets.org/research/dload/clear.pdf.

20. V. E. Lee, "Using Hierarchical Linear Modeling to Study Social Contexts: The Case of School Effects," *Educational Psychologist* 35:2 (2000), 140.

21. "About FairTest," FairTest: The National Center for Fair & Open Testing Web site, http://www.fairtest.org/Who%20We%20Are.html.

22. "What's Wrong with the NCAA's Test Score Requirements?" FairTest: The National Center for Fair & Open Testing Web site, http://www.fairtest.org/facts/prop48.htm.

SUGGESTED READING

Cameron, Mindy. "If We Set the Bar High, Our Children Will Compete." *Seattle Times,* 2 November 1997.

Crouse, James, and Dale Trusheim. *The Case against the SAT.* Chicago: University of Chicago Press, 1988.

Everson, Howard T., and Roger E. Millsap. "Beyond Individual Differences: Exploring School Effects on SAT Scores." College Board Research Report no. 2004–3, 2004.

Gould, Stephen Jay. *The Mismeasure of Man.* New York: Norton, 1996.

Hackett, R. K., Holland, P., Pearlman, M., & Thayer, D. *Test Construction Manipulating Score Difference between Black and White Examinees: Properties of the Resulting Tests.* Princeton, N.J.: Educational Testing Service, February 1987.

Jencks, Christopher, and Meredith Phillips, eds. *The Black-White Test Score Gap.* Washington, D.C.: Brookings Institution, 1998.

Kohn, Alfie. *The Case against Standardized Testing: Raising the Scores, Ruining the Schools.* New York: Heineman, 2000.

Lee, V. E. "Using Hierarchical Linear Modeling to Study Social Contexts: The Case of School Effects." *Educational Psychologist* 35:2 (2000), 125–141.

Lemann, Nicholas. *The Big Test: The Secret History of the American Meritocracy.* New York: Farrar, Straus and Giroux, 1999.

Richardson, Ken. *The Making of Intelligence.* New York: Columbia University Press, 2000.

Sacks, Peter. *Standardized Minds: The High Price of America's Testing Culture and What We Can Do to Change It.* Cambridge, Mass.: Perseus, 1999.

"Test Service Accepts Safeguards against Bias." *New York Times,* 29 November 1984.

"Variables Play Role in Races' Achievement Gap." *Atlanta Journal-Constitution,* 2 September 2004.

Zieky, Michael. "Ensuring Fairness in Licensing Exams." Educational Testing Service Web site, Winter 2002, http://www.ets.org/research/dload/clear.pdf.

Zwick, Rebecca. *Fair Game? The Use of Standardized Admissions Tests in Higher Education.* New York: RoutledgeFalmer, 2002.

Videos

ABC News. *Standardized Tests: Assessing the Price of Failure.* 21 min. 2003. Seeks to understand the ramifications of high-stakes advancement and exit exams—tests that are being used to measure schools' effectiveness, to allocate funding, and to shape the future of the nation's children.

Dickson, Deborah. *Lalee's Kin.* 2001. Explores Lalee Wallace, a great-grandmother struggling to hold her world together in the face of dire poverty in the Mississippi Delta, and Reggie Barnes, superintendent of the embattled West Tallahatchie school system. Barnes was hired as superintendent of schools in West Tallahatchie in an effort to get the school district off probation, where it was placed by the Mississippi Department of Education because of poor student performance on the Iowa Test for Basic Skills. If Barnes fails to raise the school from its current Level 1 status to Level 2, the state of Mississippi has threatened to take it over. Barnes and his faculty oppose this, fearing that administrators in far-off Jackson would not do as well in addressing the special needs of their community.

Discovery Times Channel. *Making the Grade*. 60 min. 2001.

PBS *Frontline*. "Secrets of the SAT." 60 min. 1999.

PBS *Frontline*. "The Merrow Report: Testing Our Schools." 60 min. 2002.

Web Sites

ACT Assessment, Inc., http://www.act.org.

Applied Research Center's ERASE Initiative, http://www.arc.org/erase/index.html.

The College Board, http://www.collegeboard.com.

CRESST: National Center for Research on Evaluation, Standards, and Student Teaching Web site, http://www.cse.ucla.edu/index6.htm.

Educational Testing Service, http://www.ets.org.

FairTest, http://www.fairtest.org.

Frontline, "Secrets of the SAT," http://www.pbs.org/wgbh/pages/frontline/shows/sats/.

7

WELFARE TO WORK

During the presidential election campaign of 1980, challenger Ronald Reagan highlighted government welfare programs as one of the chief differences between the incumbent, President Jimmy Carter, and himself. In particular, Reagan focused on the inefficient delivery of services by the government as well as the very philosophy of giving away money to individuals who had the ability to find work. By raising that issue, Reagan revived a dormant attitude of Americans that government aid programs were more harmful than beneficial. Only in the 1960s had that long-held mindset given way to the War on Poverty, which engineered a massive expansion of government aid programs.

To make his case, Reagan zeroed in on abusers of the system. Reagan talked often about the "Chicago welfare queen" who had "eighty names, thirty addresses, twelve Social Security cards," and received government benefits for "four non-existing deceased husbands." Reagan claimed that she had bilked the government out of $150,000. Though he did not intend to make the issue a matter of race—in particular, whites versus blacks—just discussing welfare meant that the debate might very well devolve into that type of controversy. Critics charged that Reagan had made a gross exaggeration, given that the woman was convicted of using only two aliases and committing benefit fraud of $8,000. But that criticism missed the mark, for what Reagan had done—intentionally or not—was propagate a stereotype of African American women that had become especially prevalent after the War on Poverty. Though Reagan never indicated that the woman was black, the effect of the oft-repeated story was to rouse support against abusers of the system and against the welfare and food stamps programs in general. That African Americans were disproportionate recipients of federal aid made them the target of that ire. Powerful stereotypes, built upon generations of racism and political efforts to limit government aid, had reached the pinnacle of power in the country.[1]

Two facts made the comments by Reagan especially illustrative of the welfare reform debate: first, government welfare programs have been controversial throughout American history; and second, since the beginning of government welfare programs, African Americans have constituted a disproportionate share of the recipients. Since 1970, the percentage of welfare recipients who are black has ranged between 44 and 57 percent, while African Americans constitute 12 percent of the nation's population. Issues already covered in this book—the legacy of slavery, historically poor educational opportunities, and racism—all contributed to that development. Consequently, African Americans find themselves at the center of an important policy debate that has occasionally descended into the perpetuation of stereotypes about them and their culture. Social scientist Sanford Schram, who specializes in race and welfare, has explored the persistent thinking that welfare "is largely a 'black program' needed because African Americans are trapped in a 'black underclass,' mired in a 'culture of poverty' bereft of 'personal responsibility,' and unable to break out of an intergenerational cycle of 'welfare dependency.'"[2] Such persistent stereotypes, Schram and others argue, tend to obscure the valid public policy debate over the benefits of requiring welfare recipients to work. This chapter investigates whether recent attempts to reform welfare—especially the 1996 so-called welfare-to-work law—are effective ways of improving the quality of lives for welfare recipients, or if such policies are based on stereotypes that continue to limit the ability of many African Americans to move out of poverty.

HISTORICAL CONTEXT

For much of the nation's history, social welfare programs in the United States rested with individuals and local governments. The modern question of government-run versus privately operated programs was as much a controversy in the eighteenth and nineteenth centuries as it is now; the only difference was that during those earlier periods, the debate occurred at the local rather than national level. During the formative years of the early republic, municipal governments struggled with which entity—government or private groups—could deliver welfare services most efficiently. For example, in 1788 Philadelphia ended its 20-year experiment with privately run poor relief. The operator of the program, the Quaker Bettering House, was deemed ineffective at delivering services. This spirit was not unique, either. In 1797, noted American essayist Thomas Paine, whose pamphlet *Common Sense* helped to ignite the American Revolution, wrote a new pamphlet on social welfare. Paine's *Agrarian Justice* called for the federal government to provide every person a one-time payment at age 21 and an annual payment to every individual aged 50 and older.[3] Though not adopted, and barely taken seriously at the time, Paine's ideas would eventually form the basis of the American welfare state.

Nonetheless, individual citizens continued to form their own relief organizations. During the late eighteenth and early nineteenth centuries, a bevy of poor-relief groups cropped up, especially in large cities such as Philadelphia and Baltimore. By the 1820s, a growing number of Americans determined that poverty was related to intemperance, or alcohol abuse. That habit, according to the prevailing thought, led one to become lazy and therefore prevented people from working. Thus, in a debate whose contours were not all that dissimilar from the modern controversy over welfare-to-work programs, the nineteenth-century solution to poverty was to combine temperance, or anti-alcohol, efforts with poor relief. Because individual citizens and groups started these efforts—as opposed to government sponsoring such programs—social welfare continued to be provided at the local level.

Following the Civil War, the debate over social welfare exploded onto the national stage. Rather than focusing on the poor, the controversy centered on pensions for Civil War veterans and their widows. While the vast majority of Americans supported the financial support of the war generation, two limitations to this effort prevented it from evolving into a large-scale, national welfare program. First, certain politicians supported the veterans' pension proposal for purely political reasons as opposed to a sincere desire to begin constructing a safety net for poor people that would be sponsored by the federal government. Second, the robust economic growth of the country did little to dispel earlier notions that poor people in some way deserved their status. The imagery of personal sacrifice—personified so well by Civil War veterans and their widows—served to keep poor-relief efforts in the realm of private organizations and local governments.[4]

The quick pace of industrialization during the late nineteenth century not only ushered in tremendous economic growth, but also left a growing number of Americans dissatisfied with the uneven share of wealth gained by that growth. In the political arena, the result of this dissatisfaction emerged as the Progressive movement. Progressives saw a much larger role for the federal government in improving working conditions and the quality of life for all Americans. Though they tended to concentrate on issues such as breaking up monopolies and cleaning up filthy cities, some Progressives were active at the state and national levels in constructing a poor-relief program run by the government. The success of their efforts was limited—particularly at the federal level—but did lay the foundation for eventual successes in the 1960s. During the 1910s, almost every state created pension funds for poor widows; unlike the Civil War veterans' legislation, the only requirement for receiving assistance was being a woman, widowed, and poor.[5] Not surprisingly, the first national welfare program would also focus on women and children.

Though that program would not be created until the 1960s, the interlude between the Progressive Era and that period was momentous for welfare program creation. The onset of the Great Depression in 1929 dramatically expanded the number of Americans in need of financial assistance. Farmers—many of them African Americans—saw prices plummet. Urban workers, an increasing proportion of whom were black, saw employment opportunities dwindle and wages decline. Consequently, the traditional venues for poor relief—individual organizations and municipal governments—were overwhelmed by demand. Quite simply, their resources were too scarce to meet the need. As the depression grew deeper, the political pressure on President Herbert Hoover to initiate government-sponsored relief was intense. Finally, in 1932, Hoover pushed through Congress the Emergency Relief Act, which gave states $300 million in loans to supplement local relief efforts. By the next year, 60 percent of all relief efforts in the United States were funded by the federal government.[6]

With Hoover's successor, Franklin Roosevelt, came a mandate to continue the expanded role of the federal government in providing social welfare. In 1933, Congress created the Federal Emergency Relief Program, which provided even more direct relief assistance to state and local governments. But the suspicious attitude toward the poor by previous generations had not disappeared completely. Public concern over giving the needy direct relief mounted. In response, President Roosevelt searched for solutions that would both address the need of the country's poor while preventing the development of an expectation by the poor that government must be the answer to their problems. The first such effort, created in late 1933, was the Civil Works Administration. Though the agency would be short-lived because of concern by business owners, it provided a foundation upon which subsequent indirect relief efforts would be based.[7]

The succeeding agency, the Works Progress Administration, was much better received and therefore more successful. Created in 1935, the WPA was a massive government public works program that gave many poor Americans what they needed desperately—a job—while making them earn that assistance. In the same vein, Congress decided four years later to limit the time that an individual could participate in the WPA. Basically the welfare reform of the 1930s, the new 18-month time limit on an individual's participation in the WPA job program cut 775,000 people from the rolls by 1940; only 100,000 of them found jobs within three months.[8] Foreshadowing almost exactly the welfare-to-work debates of the late twentieth and early twenty-first centuries, this limitation to a large New Deal program perpetuated the long-held belief against direct, no-strings-attached poor relief by the government.

At the same time that the Works Progress Administration was being reduced in size, the federal government created the first national social welfare program. But because this program could be used only by poor women and their children, it fit within that mindset of most Americans that only those two groups were worthy of direct aid (the Social Security Administration was created in 1935 to provide old-age insurance to the nation's older citizens). By the end of 1940, Aid to Dependent Children provided 360,000 families with $18 per month for the first child and $12 per month for each additional child (Social Security recipients received $30 per month). But World War II, which spurred tremendous economic growth at home, made unemployment and poverty dramatically low. Thus, in the immediate postwar years, the program's rolls grew slowly, and the nation maintained its commitment to only limited direct aid to poor families.[9]

The turning point in the history of welfare came in the 1960s. Continued high rates of poverty—particularly among African Americans—convinced President Lyndon Johnson that the federal government had to expand its role in providing assistance to the nation's poor. A central facet of Johnson's War on Poverty was expanding Aid to Dependent Children in 1965. Larger and renamed, Aid to Families with Dependent Children (AFDC) grew by approximately 800,000 families by the end of the decade. Related programs, such as the Work Incentive Program (WIN), perpetuated the traditional notion of work for assistance.[10] Even with new developments such as AFDC, the belief that "workfare" was a more effective policy than "welfare" remained popular.

In substantive terms, President Reagan was determined to "trim the safety net," which meant scaling back the size and costs of programs such as AFDC.[11] Reagan and his conservative allies, while targeting new programs, were merely advocating a position against direct government aid that had been prevalent since the eighteenth century. Though Reagan never enjoyed enough support in Congress for the full implementation of his less-expensive safety net idea, he was able to tweak the system. Most prominently, in 1988, he pushed through Congress the Job Opportunities and Basic Skills (JOBS) Act, which was designed to assist the poor in moving from welfare to work. The capstone of Reagan's welfare reform, JOBS proved to be ineffective at reducing welfare's rolls.[12] Both the push for reform and stereotypes of so-called welfare queens continued to dominate the national conversation over welfare reform.

By the mid-1990s, angst over welfare had reached a fever pitch. Both supporters and detractors of government-sponsored direct aid saw inherent problems in the system. Reformers argued that the largesse of the program—as exemplified by Reagan's welfare queen—was not only inefficient but also promoted immoral lifestyles. Supporters of welfare rebuffed such claims and charged that if indeed welfare was not as efficient as possible, it was a result of benefits not keeping up with inflation, thereby reducing the purchasing power of government aid for individual recipients. In 1996, as President Bill Clinton prepared for his reelection campaign, he made comprehensive welfare reform the cornerstone of his domestic agenda. Meshing well with the interests of the new Republican majority in Congress, Clinton succeeded in pushing through the Personal Responsibility and Work Opportunity Reconciliation Act. Discussed in detail in the following section, this legislation was the first overhaul of the system since Lyndon Johnson and Congress expanded AFDC in 1965. At the root of the legislation—and subsequent debates over its reauthorization—is whether welfare to work is an effective means of helping poor families. Not surprisingly, the issue of African American stereotypes remains a central part of the debate.

Temporary Assistance for Needy Families

President Clinton and the new Republican leadership in Congress struck a bipartisan chord when they committed themselves to reforming welfare. Promising to "end welfare as we know it," Clinton called for an updated AFDC program that would apply rigorous work requirements to its recipients.[13] The result, Temporary Assistance for Needy Families (TANF), is a block grant created by the Personal Responsibility and Work Opportunity Reconciliation Act of 1996. TANF completely replaced the Aid to Families with Dependent Children (AFDC) program, which had provided cash welfare to poor families with children since 1935.

As a block grant program, TANF gives states considerable leeway in how they administer the funds. States can use TANF money to meet any of the four purposes set out in federal law, which are to "provide assistance to needy families so that children can be cared for at home; to end the dependence of needy parents on government benefits by promoting job preparation, work and marriage; to prevent and reduce the incidence of out-of-wedlock pregnancies; and to encourage the formation and maintenance of two-parent families."[14] States have used their TANF funds in a variety of ways, including cash assistance (including wage supplements), child care, education and job training, transportation, and a variety of other services to help families make the transition to work. In addition, to receive TANF funds, states must spend some of their own money on programs for needy families.

States have broad discretion to determine who will be eligible for various TANF-funded benefits and services. The main federal requirement is that states use the funds to serve families with children. A state can set different eligibility tests for different programs funded by the TANF block grant. For example, a state could choose to limit TANF cash assistance to very poor families but provide TANF-funded child care or transportation assistance to working families with somewhat higher incomes.[15]

Two key elements of state TANF programs are work requirements and time limits, both of which apply to basic assistance (cash and other assistance designed to meet basic ongoing needs). Federal law requires that half of the families receiving assistance under TANF be engaged in some kind of work-related activity for at least 30 hours a week. States get credits for reduced case-loads, however, and are required to have fewer than half of families engaged in federally defined work activities. Nonetheless, states have generally exceeded the minimum federal requirements for the number of families participating in work activities. On time limits, the general rule is that no family may receive federally funded assistance for longer than five years. States are allowed to use federal TANF dollars to extend time limits, but only so long as no more than 20 percent of the caseload has exhausted the five-year limit. While about 20 states have established time limits shorter than five years, states often provide exemptions and exemptions for some groups of families meeting specified criteria.[16]

The law that created the TANF block grant authorized funding through the end of federal fiscal year 2002 (September 30, 2002). In 1997, only one year after he signed the welfare-to-work legislation, President Bill Clinton concluded, "I think it's fair to say the debate is over. We now know that welfare reform works."[17] While many Americans agree with that assessment, there has been enough disagreement to delay the permanent reauthorization of TANF. Since 2002, Congress has been working on legislation to reauthorize the block grant and make some modifications to the rules and funding levels. However, no final agreement has yet been reached on reauthorization legislation. In the meantime, TANF funding has been temporarily extended several times. Thus, the current debate over welfare reform is very relevant, as both supporters and opponents see opportunities to advance their positions during reauthorization battles in Congress.[18]

Woman practices her typing skills in Cleveland as part of the Welfare-to-Work program, 1997 (AP Wide World Photo/Tony Dejak).

FRAMING THE ISSUE

Prior to TANF's passage in 1996, much of the debate over welfare reform was theoretical. With the welfare-to-work program having been in place for several years, however, the contemporary debate tends to focus on the effectiveness of that legislation. Nonetheless, the philosophical arguments by supporters and opponents of welfare reform remain prominent and central to the debate. Supporters of welfare reform base their position on five main arguments. First, supporters argue that no government—federal, state, or local—should give away money to able-bodied individuals without those recipients having to work in return. Supporters claim that this practice violates a central facet of human and American life that one should earn his or her station in life. Second, by devising programs that provide assistance with no requirement for work, such policies create something that reform supporters call a culture of dependence. By not requiring work for assistance, welfare programs create a disincentive for recipients to be proactive in searching for employment. This stamping out of personal initiative, according to supporters, creates a problem—abuse—that forms their third distinct argument in favor of welfare reform. Though Ronald Reagan's welfare queen story was an exaggeration, the reality was, nonetheless, that the woman in question had abused the system in order to receive more assistance. In a culture of dependence, such abuse of the system should not be surprising, supporters say. Fourth, welfare programs made worse the existing problem of out-of-wedlock births, which merely perpetuated the cycle of poverty and dependence on government assistance. For supporters of reform, many of whom are politically conservative, this possible effect of welfare programs on families has been pivotal in their support of reform. Finally, especially given all of the problems just listed, supporters maintain that government-sponsored welfare programs are too expensive.

Opponents of reform also base their position on five distinct arguments. First, they contend, reform advocates have based much of their proposals on a damaging stereotype of African Americans. Opponents often cite statistics that illustrate a higher number of white families receiving assistance through welfare programs (although, as mentioned previously, African Americans form a higher *percentage* of recipients than their share of the nation's population). The most active welfare reform opponents go so far as to suggest that welfare reform is merely a masked way to prevent the economic progress of African Americans. Second, critics of welfare reform argue that welfare recipients are insufficiently trained and educated to earn higher-paying jobs. Consequently, they must take jobs that pay at or near minimum wage, which many times provide a standard of living lower than that of government assistance. Therefore, opponents argue, the disincentive lies in the type of work available. Third, because of state variations to the national welfare-to-work law, a wide disparity in standards exists across the country. For example, in Wisconsin, welfare recipients can stay on welfare for only 18 months, while recipients in Oregon have twice that long to find employment. The policy has therefore not ensured fairness, according to opponents. Fourth, reform opponents rail against the idea that marriage is the solution to poverty. They argue that reform advocates exaggerated the number of welfare recipients who had more children in order to receive more benefits and suggest that job training and education would be more important than efforts to support traditional marriage. Finally, opponents of welfare reform argue that the free market is not always better than government. The same cost overruns and inefficiency that reform supporters say were rife in the government programs also exist in some privatized, state-level programs.[19]

Obviously, there is little common ground on this issue among supporters and opponents. A closer examination of their positions, as well as of some key leaders on each side, will indicate why.

SUPPORTERS OF WELFARE REFORM

Advocates of welfare reform see it not only as an important policy in and of itself, but also one that has other benefits. Helping welfare recipients earn gainful employment, according to reform supporters, leads to greater stability among families. Supporters contend that the policy also helps to break the cycle of poverty and government aid, meaning that children of recipients do not necessarily have to become similarly attached to government aid.

A significant amount of recent research seems to bear out that conclusion. One study concluded that in terms of education and earnings potential as adults, children with parents on welfare lagged far behind children in poor families who did not receive welfare assistance. Moreover, the report argued that "children from welfare-dependent families tend to have lower levels of cognitive development and are more likely to drop out of school." In short, supporters of welfare reform contend that welfare exacerbates existing problems among poor families, especially poor African American families, and that the 1996 TANF is an important start to solving this problem permanently.[20]

With several years' research now available to ascertain the effects of TANF on particular groups, such as African American children, reform supporters have marshaled that evidence to make their case. The research report found that since welfare reform, approximately 1.2 million African American children have moved out of poverty. Moreover, the study found that since 1996, for every black child whose economic circumstances worsened, six black children have seen substantial improvements in their economic status. While opponents of welfare reform credit the pronounced economic growth during that span, supporters argue that without welfare reform, the improved economic conditions for black families would have been considerably worse, or even nonexistent.[21]

The Heritage Foundation

Reform proposals like welfare to work often become reality because of the efforts by think tanks, or policy research and advocacy groups. One such group, the Heritage Foundation, is the major conservative think tank in the country. During the debates over TANF in 1996, and during subsequent legislative battles to reauthorize the law, the Heritage Foundation has exerted considerable pressure through research, lobbying, and conferences that highlight the continuing need and successes of welfare reform.

The Heritage Foundation has been most concerned with how welfare reform has had a positive impact on recipients and their families. The organization cites a bevy of research data to underscore its case. For example, a 2003 Heritage report found that since the passage of TANF in 1996, the unemployment rate of poor, single mothers decreased from 33 percent to nearly 0 percent.[22] Welfare reform has also spurred significant improvement in poverty rates among single mothers.

Researchers at the Heritage Foundation have also concluded that welfare reform, rather than the national economic expansion of the 1990s, accounts for declining poverty rates and a decreasing caseload (number of families on government assistance) for TANF. In spite of the eight periods of economic expansion between 1950 and 1991, none of those growth periods caused a significant decrease in the number of families receiving AFDC benefits. The only period of economic expansion in which the caseload decline was appreciable was the late 1990s, when TANF was created. Thus, even with dark predictions that TANF would push at least one million children into poverty, 2.3 million fewer children live in poverty today than there were in 1996. One Heritage Foundation report shows that "the poverty rates of both black children and children of single mothers have been cut by one-third and are now at the lowest points in U.S. history."[23]

By providing welfare reform advocates with an influential research arm, the Heritage Foundation had an important role in the passage of TANF. As debates over continued reauthorization of the law continue, the influence of Heritage on the issue of welfare reform will only increase.

Star Parker

Equally influential on the matter of reforming welfare is writer and social policy consultant Star Parker. An African American and a former welfare mother, Parker has used her transition from poverty to national activist experiences as the crux of her arguments against government assistance and for welfare reform. Her recent book on the subject, *Uncle Sam's Plantation: How Big Government Enslaves the Poor and What We Can Do About It*, equates government programs such as welfare with modern-day slavery. Not surprisingly, Parker has attracted both acclaim and criticism for her sharp commentary on the issue.[24]

Parker pulls no punches when criticizing welfare. "Government programs," she says, "were supposed to lift up the poor. Blacks have paid a dear price for buying into this. Forty years ago, the black community was poor in resources but rich in spirit. The black family was relatively intact. Today, as a result of a generation of blacks being taught that they can't take care of themselves, most black children are born to unwed mothers and grow up in broken homes."[25] In addition to indicting government-sponsored welfare as actually a problem—rather than merely an ineffective solution—Parker echoes the sentiment of many supporters of welfare reform. Most controversially, Parker equates those programs with modern-day slavery. "Poverty programs," Parker argues, "enslave the poor in government-run housing projects, government health care, government food stamps, government child care facilities and government schools. Is it any wonder so many poor children end up in government prisons?"[26]

In addition to her writing and speaking, Star Parker founded the Coalition on Urban Renewal and Education (CURE), an organization that focuses on race and poverty in the media, inner-city neighborhoods, and public policy. CURE was instrumental in developing and passing TANF, and Parker lobbied diligently for time limits and work requirements to be part of the law. Since the TANF debate, CURE has consulted with political leaders on how to develop social policies that encourage individual merit and personal responsibility. It has also developed significant outreach efforts in poor neighborhoods including an annual empowerment conference, training clinics, inner-city town hall meetings, and church lecture series. As a major player in the welfare reform debate, CURE will remain influential as reauthorization discussions continue.

OPPONENTS OF WELFARE REFORM

Critics of TANF, and of welfare reform in general, are dubious about the government taking a less active and less expensive role in the lives of poor Americans. This position is especially relevant to African Americans, given the history of racism and segregation that government action finally began to improve. Thus, opponents of welfare reform tend to couch their arguments in terms that highlight a potential social disaster that might impact African Americans disproportionately. Wary of the stereotypes often used to justify welfare reform—most of which refer to black women—opponents have tried to regroup since TANF's passage. Most recently, they have begun to exert political pressure on Congress to ease work requirements and time limits that are mandated by TANF.

Although the House of Representatives passed a bill in 2002 that expanded the work requirements portion of TANF, the bill has yet to be passed by the Senate because of considerable pressure by opponents. One House member, Jose Serrano of New York, has highlighted the problems with both TANF and the new bill. "If self-sufficiency can be defined as raising a family just on or below the poverty level, with little or no chance of increasing earning potential because the breadwinner is not equipped with competitive education or job training, then I agree with my colleagues that 1996 welfare reform has been a success," Serrano argues. Because the average job acquired by welfare recipients pays only $6.61 per hour and offers no health benefits, requiring recipients to work 40 hours per week is "counterproductive to finding a long-term solution to poverty." Rather than continue this misguided policy, Serrano and most opponents of welfare to work want the government to invest in better education for poor Americans, especially African Americans and Hispanics.[27]

The Urban Institute

An important counterpart to the Heritage Foundation is the Urban Institute. As a liberal think tank, the Urban Institute is active on a host of issues, but it has been one of the lead research and advocacy groups who are opposed to welfare reform. Like many reform opponents, the Urban Institute has focused on the effects of welfare reform on African Americans.

A recent research study by the Urban Institute concluded that TANF and other welfare reform proposals "could more accurately be described as a Trojan horse designed to dismantle the welfare state that has existed for the past 60 years." This report calls into question the motives of welfare reformers, in particular by dismissing the effects of programs such as TANF. The Urban Institute faults efforts at welfare reform because of limited change in other areas, such as the minimum wage and health insurance, that would make the work requirements more feasible. The report concludes, "If the objective is to reduce poverty without encouraging dependency, the most important thing that government can do is to assist low-income working families with such measures as the EITC [Earned Income Tax Credit], child care, subsidized health insurance, and adjustments in the minimum wage." While not critical of inducing welfare recipients to work, the Urban Institute questions the sufficiency of reform thus far. "If personal commitments to work and family are the surest way out of poverty, as they have been in the past," the organization's researchers conclude, "then these work-oriented measures are the best way to keep those who play by the rules from falling further behind."[28]

An entirely distinct set of research has focused on the impact of welfare to work on families who left welfare. The Urban Institute has sponsored a number of these studies, all of which indicate that the picture is not nearly as rosy as reform advocates have suggested. One study by the organization concluded that "among adolescent boys, those in leaver families [families who left welfare] were more likely than those in current recipient families to have a high level of behavioral and emotional problems, to have skipped school twice or more in the previous year, to have been suspended or expelled from school in the previous year, and to be poorly engaged in school." Because these were four precise areas in which welfare reform was supposed to help poor families, the results thus far have been disappointing, say Urban Institute scholars. They conclude, "Not only did adolescent leaver boys fare worse on these four indicators than did adolescent current recipient boys, but the adolescent leaver boys were also more likely to be at risk on these indicators than were adolescent girls in leaver families."[29] With results as negative as these, the organization remains firmly opposed to TANF and has urged continued efforts to "reform the reform."

Betty Reid Mandell

Opponents of welfare reform do not have a lead spokesperson with the notoriety of Star Parker, but they do have a handful of heavyweight activists. One of them is Betty Reid Mandell, a welfare rights activist since the 1960s. Mandell founded and co-edits *Survival News,* a journal that focuses on the plight of poor Americans. Mandell, a retired sociology professor, has also authored several books and articles on social welfare, many of which address the problems that welfare reform imposes on African American families.[30]

Mandell's most effective strategy is her use of specific people as case studies to illustrate the problems of welfare reform. She has written often about specific people, usually African American women, whose situations defy the statistical evidence of reform supporters. Ranging from quirks in the bureaucratic process to worker incompetence, reasons for the plight of these individuals do not include their own lack of desire to better their condition, Mandell argues. She chafes at reformers' assertions that TANF has succeeded in dramatically reducing the number of people on welfare. "One of the most common reasons for case closings during welfare reform has been sanctions by the welfare department," Mandell contends. "A client may be sanctioned from the rolls for any of a number of bureaucratic reasons. Clients are sanctioned for failing to return a form on time, for failing to fill a form out correctly, for not coming to a meeting with a worker (even when the meeting conflicted with required community service activities), for not cooperating with work or community service requirements, and often because of the worker's mistake."[31]

Mandell has been relentless in her indictment of welfare reform as scaling back the progress on poverty that began in the 1960s. She contends that since welfare reform in 1996, "States have stripped more than a million low-income American parents, mostly single women, of health insurance." Moreover, TANF has had an effect on many other social welfare programs not covered by the law. For example, Mandell argues, "Welfare reform has also reduced the number of people who receive food stamps. States have been neglecting to tell people that they are still eligible for food stamps when they leave the welfare rolls, and many people who have not been on welfare don't realize that they are eligible." Since 1994, according to Mandell, 11 million fewer Americans receive food stamps, a decline that she attributes to an increased hostility toward people receiving government aid.[32]

Clearly, if Betty Reid Mandell is correct, long-held beliefs that government should not provide direct financial assistance have once again become prevalent. While problematic from the vantage point of welfare reform's opponents, the reappearance of that mindset would be welcomed by reform advocates. As Congress once again grapples with reauthorization and possible revision of TANF, the debate will only grow louder. As with the other issues covered in this book, welfare reform places African Americans at the center of a pivotal national policy debate. The shape that the debate and policy take in coming years depends largely on the powerful stereotypes of African Americans, which is the subject of chapter 8.

QUESTIONS AND ACTIVITIES

1. Organize your class into two groups. One group will support government-sponsored welfare; the other will not. Debate the issue. To add a wrinkle to your debate, put yourselves in specific time periods, such as 1780–1820, 1840–1870, 1890–1920, 1930–1940, the 1960s, and today. How do your arguments change according to the major events and ideas of each period? What arguments remain the same?

2. Research the welfare programs of other countries. What features are similar to and different from the welfare system in the United States? Why do you think those similarities and differences exist?

3. Research how individual states have used money provided from Temporary Assistance for Needy Families. What does your state do? How does your state compare with the others? Has there been any local news coverage in your area about TANF? The reauthorization of TANF? Welfare or welfare reform generally?

4. Imagine that you are in Congress and that your constituents want you to update TANF. They have given you few specifics, so you have considerable leeway in what you do. What do you propose? Are your proposals feasible—that is, will they be enacted, and will they change TANF positively?

5. In what other public policy issues are nonfacts such as stereotypes persuasive parts of the debate?

NOTES

1. "The Mendacity Index," *Washington Monthly,* September 2003.

2. Sanford F. Schram, "Putting a Black Face on Welfare: The Good and the Bad," in *Race and the Politics of Welfare Reform,* ed. Sanford F. Schram, Joe Soss, and Richard C. Fording (Ann Arbor: University of Michigan Press, 2003), 196.

3. Seth Rockman, *Welfare Reform in the Early Republic: A Brief History with Documents* (Boston: Bedford/St. Martin's, 2003), 5–7, 165.

4. Theda Skocpol, *Protecting Soldiers and Mothers: The Political Origins of Social Policy in the United States* (Boston: Harvard University Press, 1992), 102–51.

5. Charles Noble, *Welfare As We Knew It: A Political History of the American Welfare State* (Oxford: Oxford University Press, 1997), 36–53.

6. Nancy E. Rose, "Historicizing Government Work Programs: A Spectrum from Workfare to Fair Work," Center for Full Employment and Price Stability Seminar Paper no. 2, March 2000, http://www.cfeps.org/pubs/sp/sp2/.

7. Noble, *Welfare,* 70–73.

8. Rose, "Historicizing."

9. Susan W. Blank and Barbara B. Blum, "A Brief History of Work Expectations for Welfare Mothers," The Future of Children Web site, http://www.futureofchildren. org/information2826/information_show.htm?doc_id=72241.

10. Rose, "Historicizing."

11. Martin Gilens, "How the Poor Became Black: The Racialization of American Poverty in the Mass Media," in *Race and the Politics of Welfare Reform,* ed. Sanford F. Schram, Joe Soss, and Richard C. Fording, (Ann Arbor: University of Michigan Press, 2003), 118.

12. Richard C. Fording, "'Laboratories of Democracy' or Symbolic Politics? The Racial Origins of Welfare Reform," in *Race and the Politics of Welfare Reform,* ed. Sanford F. Schram, Joe Soss, and Richard C. Fording (Ann Arbor: University of Michigan Press, 2003), 76.

13. Hugh Heclo, "The Politics of Welfare Reform," in *The New World of Welfare,* ed. Rebecca Blank and Ron Haskins (Washington, D.C.: Brookings Institution Press, 2001), 187–89.

14. "Aid to Families with Dependent Children (AFDC) and Temporary Assistance for Needy Families (TANF): Overview," Assistant Secretary for Planning and Education Web site, http://www.aspe.hhs.gov/hsp/abbrev/afdc-tanf.htm.

15. Ron Haskins and Rebecca M. Blank, "Welfare Reform: An Agenda for Reauthorization," in *The New World of Welfare,* ed. Rebecca Blank and Ron Haskins, 6–15 (Washington, D.C.: Brookings Institution Press, 2001).

16. Ibid.

17. Alan Weil and Kenneth Finegold, eds., *Welfare Reform: The Next Act* (Washington, D.C.: Urban Institute Press, 1998), 1.

18. Patricia L. Kirk, "Running Out of Time: Congress Considers TANF Reauthorization as Some Native Recipients Face the End of Benefits," *American Indian Report* 20 (June 2004): 12–17.

19. An excellent synopsis of the welfare reform opponents' position is "The False Foundations of Welfare Reform," *Applied Research Center Web site,* February 2001, http://www.arc.org/downloads/false_found.pdf.

20. Robert Rector and Patrick Fagan, "How Welfare Harms Kids," Heritage Foundation Backgrounder no. 1048, 5 June 1996.

21. Melissa G. Pardue, "Sharp Reduction in Black Child Poverty Due to Welfare Reform," Heritage Foundation Web site, 12 June 2003, http://www.heritage.org/ Research/Welfare/BG1661.cfm.

22. Robert Rector and Patrick Fagan, "The Continuing Good News About Welfare Reform," Heritage Foundation Backgrounder no. 1620, 6 February 2003.

23. Ibid.

24. Star Parker, *Uncle Sam's Plantation: How Big Government Enslaves the Poor and What We Can Do About It* (Nashville, Tenn.: WND Books, 2003).

25. Star Parker, "Politicians Fawn over 'Ordinary' Americans," *USA Today,* 19 December 2003.

26. Star Parker, "Time for Next Steps in Welfare Reform," *USA Today,* 6 August 1999.

27. "Black, Hispanic Caucuses Take Aim at Welfare Bill," *Black Issues in Higher Education,* 20 June 2002.

28. Isabel V. Sawhill, "Welfare Reform: An Analysis of the Issues," Urban Institute Web site, 1 May 1995, http://www.urban.org/Template.cfm?NavMenuID=24&template=/TaggedContent/ViewPublication.cfm&PublicationID=5872.

29. Sharon Vandivere, Martha Zaslow, Jennifer Brooks, and Zakia Redd, "Do Child Characteristics Affect How Children Fare in Families Receiving and Leaving Welfare?" August 2004 Discussion Paper, part of *Assessing New Federalism* series (Washington: Urban Institute, 2004), 28–29.

30. For example, see Betty Reid Mandell, ed., *Welfare in America: Controlling the "Dangerous Classes"* (Englewood Cliffs, N.J.: Prentice-Hall, 1975).

31. Betty Reid Mandell, "Welfare Reform: The War against the Poor," *New Politics* 8:2 (Winter 2001), 3.

32. Ibid, 6.

SUGGESTED READING

"Aid to Families with Dependent Children (AFDC) and Temporary Assistance for Needy Families (TANF): Overview." Assistant Secretary for Planning and Education Web site, http://www.aspe.hhs.gov/hsp/abbrev/afdc-tanf.htm.

Albelda, Randy, and Ann Withorn. *Lost Ground: Welfare Reform, Poverty, and Beyond.* Cambridge, Mass.: SouthEnd Press, 2002.

"Black, Hispanic Caucuses Take Aim at Welfare Bill." *Black Issues in Higher Education,* 20 June 2002.

Blank, Susan W., and Barbara B. Blum. "A Brief History of Work Expectations for Welfare Mothers." Future of Children Web site, http://www.futureofchildren.org/information2826/information_show.htm?doc_id=72241.

Cozic, Charles P., ed. *Welfare Reform.* San Diego: Greenhaven Press, 1997.

"The False Foundations of Welfare Reform." Applied Research Center Web site, February 2001, http://www.arc.org/downloads/false_found.pdf.

Gilens, Martin. *Why Americans Hate Welfare: Race, Media, and the Politics of Antipoverty Policy.* Chicago: University of Chicago Press, 2003.

Katz, Michael. *Undeserving Poor.* New York: Pantheon Books, 1990.

Kirk, Patricia L. "Running Out of Time: Congress Considers TANF Reauthorization as Some Native Recipients Face the End of Benefits." *American Indian Report* 20 (June 2004): 12–17.

Mandell, Betty Reid, ed. *Welfare in America: Controlling the "Dangerous Classes."* Englewood Cliffs, N.J.: Prentice-Hall, 1975.

———. "Welfare Reform: The War against the Poor." *New Politics* 8 (2) (Winter 2001), 1–14.

"The Mendacity Index." *Washington Monthly,* September 2003.

Noble, Charles. *Welfare as We Knew It: A Political History of the American Welfare State*. Oxford: Oxford University Press, 1997.

Pardue, Melissa G. "Sharp Reduction in Black Child Poverty Due to Welfare Reform." Heritage Foundation Web site, 12 June 2003, http://www.heritage.org/Research/Welfare/BG1661.cfm.

Parker, Star. "Politicians Fawn over 'Ordinary' Americans." *USA Today*, 19 December 2003.

———. "Time for Next Steps in Welfare Reform." *USA Today*, 6 August 1999.

———. *Uncle Sam's Plantation: How Big Government Enslaves the Poor and What We Can Do About It*. Nashville, Tenn.: WND Books, 2003.

Quadagno, Jill. *The Color of Welfare: How Racism Undermined the War on Poverty*. New York: Oxford University Press, 1996.

Rector, Robert, and Patrick Fagan. "How Welfare Harms Kids." Heritage Foundation Backgrounder no. 1048, 5 June 1996.

Rockman, Seth. *Welfare Reform in the Early Republic: A Brief History with Documents*. Boston: Bedford/St. Martin's, 2003.

Rose, Nancy E. "Historicizing Government Work Programs: A Spectrum from Workfare to Fair Work." Center for Full Employment and Price Stability Seminar Paper no. 2, March 2000, http://www.cfeps.org/pubs/sp/sp2/.

Sawhill, Isabel V. "Welfare Reform: An Analysis of the Issues." Urban Institute Web site, 1 May 1995, http://www.urban.org/Template.cfm?NavMenuID=24&template=/TaggedContent/ViewPublication.cfm&PublicationID=5872.

Schram, Sanford F., Joe Soss, and Richard C. Fording, eds. *Race and the Politics of Welfare Reform*. Ann Arbor: University of Michigan Press, 2003.

Skocpol, Theda. *Protecting Soldiers and Mothers: The Political Origins of Social Policy in the United States*. Boston: Harvard University Press, 1992.

Vandivere, Sharon, Martha Zaslow, Jennifer Brooks, and Zakia Redd. "Do Child Characteristics Affect How Children Fare in Families Receiving and Leaving Welfare?" August 2004 Discussion Paper, part of *Assessing New Federalism* series. Washington: Urban Institute, 2004.

Weil, Alan, and Kenneth Finegold, eds. *Welfare Reform: The Next Act*. Washington, D.C.: Urban Institute Press, 1998.

Videos

Abt, Emily. *Take It From Me: Life After Welfare*. 75 min. National Women's Studies Association, 2001. The film gives people a detailed idea of what welfare recipients are up against trying to make the transition from welfare to work. It also shows that welfare reform has hardened political and social attitudes toward the poor and made the system less and less responsive to individual needs and circumstances.

Weisberg, Roger. *Ending Welfare as We Know It*. 90 min. Public Policy Productions, 1999. This film follows six welfare mothers over the course of a year as they struggle to comply with new work requirements, find reliable child care and transportation, battle drug addiction and depression, confront domestic violence, and try to make ends meet in the new era of welfare reform.

———. *Making Welfare Work.* 58 min. Public Policy Productions, 1996. While President Clinton declared his desire to "end welfare as we know it," there is little consensus over how to make welfare work. This film explores the success as well as the controversy surrounding welfare reform experiments and cautions us not to further shortchange disadvantaged families in our rush to overhaul a failing welfare system.

Web Sites

Heritage Foundation Welfare Research Web site, http://www.heritage.org/Research/Welfare/.
Low Income Networking and Communications (LINC Project) TANF Resources Web site, http://www.lincproject.org/organizing/tanf/brmarticle_.shtml.
Urban Institute, *Assessing the New Federalism,* http://www.urban.org/Content/Research/NewFederalism/AboutANF/AboutANF.htm. Contains the Welfare Rules Database, which students can use to research TANF programs in each state.
Welfare and Work Web site, Assistant Secretary for Planning and Evaluation, http://aspe.os.dhhs.gov/hsp/hspwelfare.htm.

8

———•◦∗◦•———

MEDIA STEREOTYPES

In May 2004, during the 50th anniversary commemoration of the *Brown v. Board of Education* decision, the issue of stereotypes of African Americans took center stage. In a clearly strange development, given the positive tone of Howard University's celebration of the landmark decision, the attention spent on black stereotypes was sparked by an icon of African Americans, Bill Cosby. One of the most important entertainers in modern American society, Cosby ignited a maelstrom by making pointed, seemingly accusatory comments about some black Americans. Akin to his statements about cultural assimilation (discussed in chapter 3), Cosby reserved his most severe criticism of African Americans for alleged laziness, lack of education, and contentment with impoverished surroundings. In particular, Cosby took African American parents to task. "Ladies and gentlemen," Cosby exhorted, "the lower economic people are not holding up their end in this deal. These people are not parenting. They are buying things for kids—$500 sneakers for what? And won't spend $200 for *Hooked on Phonics*."[1]

But the entertainer was not finished. He bluntly discussed another stereotype that has hung on black Americans like an albatross: a propensity to commit crime. Cosby exclaimed, "These are not political criminals. These are people going around stealing Coca-Cola. People getting shot in the back of the head over a piece of pound cake, and then we run out and we are outraged, [saying] 'The cops shouldn't have shot him.' What the hell was he doing with the pound cake in his hand?"[2] Cosby continued. "I'm talking about these people who cry when their son is standing there in an orange

Comic Bill Cosby with the Rev. Jesse Jackson, at the Rainbow
Push Coalition annual conference in Chicago, 2004. Here,
Cosby upbraided low-income blacks for squandering oppor-
tunities afforded them from the Civil Rights Movement
(AP Wide World Photo/M. Spencer Green).

[prison jumpsuit]. Where were you when he was 2? Where were you when
he was 12? Where were you when he was 18, and how come you don't know
he had a pistol?" Cosby asked.[3] The audience, composed mostly of African
Americans, did not know whether to laugh nervously or to applaud. Bill
Cosby, the longtime antistereotype, had not only expressed outrage against
other African Americans, but had also given license for others to believe that
such stereotypes are real.

In short, Cosby had touched a nerve by addressing full-bore an issue that
Americans, regardless of ethnic and racial background, had shoved away from

public dialogue. Stereotypes, which are always painful for their targets, had become especially out of fashion following the political correctness movement of the 1980s and 1990s. But the thrusting of those stereotypes onto a very public, national stage by the nation's best-known African American figure drew both applause and severe criticism. In response to that criticism, Bill Cosby remarked, "I think we're past the furor part now. It's a movement now that needs to happen.... It's time for people to just stop seeing themselves so much as victims, so much in poverty, and realize what education does and fight for it like you're fighting for your life—and you are because that's what our children are."[4]

By refusing to apologize for his comments, Bill Cosby ensured that the thorny issue of African American stereotypes would become a serious point of discussion for Americans. His supporters argue that Cosby was not perpetuating a stereotype at all but was merely highlighting some very real problems that are especially acute among African Americans. On the other hand, Cosby's critics maintain that popular stereotypes of African Americans— problems in families, laziness, excelling only in athletics—are incorrect, are racist, and perpetuate unfair characterizations of African Americans. They add that Cosby, as a black man, played into the hands of some Americans who merely want to cast African Americans in the worst possible light. By examining the arguments of each position, and by using the Bill Cosby controversy as a helpful example of the issue, this chapter unearths both the modern and historical context for what is an important national debate.

HISTORICAL CONTEXT

Stereotypes of African Americans have existed in the United States since the seventeenth century, when the first slaves from Africa were imported to Virginia and other southern colonies. These characterizations were rooted in the medieval European sensibility that black skin connoted evil, lack of Christianity, and social backwardness. The American version of those attitudes was influenced by local contexts, namely the expanding institution of slavery during the 1700s and 1800s. Describing African Americans as part of a permanent "mudsill" class, antebellum American writers cemented stereotypes that remain largely intact even in the twenty-first century.

During the period of enslavement, several stereotypes of African Americans existed. The most prevalent was that of Sambo. Used to describe black male slaves, Sambo was fraught with a host of insidious assumptions: African American slaves were naturally lazy, intellectually inferior, and inherently docile. Likewise, the stereotypical Mammy was a good-hearted but plodding caretaker of slaveowners' children. Buck was used to caricature male slaves who were sexually overactive; Jezebel was his female counterpart. Finally, and as a powerful example that some stereotypes were used internally—that is, by African Americans themselves—Tom was a slave who went along with the wishes of his master, even at the expense of his fellow slaves. All of these characteristics, according to the stereotypes, justified treating slaves like infants. In fact, as many defenders of slavery during the nineteenth century argued, whites were actually doing African Americans a favor by enslaving them, as people of African descent were allegedly prone to misconduct and social drift without guidance. This infantilization of the entire population of enslaved African Americans was thus the crucial element in rationalizing slavery's existence.[5]

But the end of slavery in 1865 did not spark an end to black stereotypes. In fact, in some ways, it strengthened them, as African Americans came to be seen by poor whites as competing laborers. Consequently, although the Sambo and Mammy stereotypes were altered to fit the new circumstances following emancipation, the root idea—that black Americans were inherently inferior—remained. Waves of hysteria often swept the South that roaming former slaves—all Bucks—were on the loose, raping white women as they traveled. Proving that stereotypes are not empty rhetoric, the ruthless lynching campaigns during the late nineteenth and early twentieth centuries were often justified by such baseless fear.[6]

By far, the most crucial spread of black stereotypes happened on the stage. Starting in the 1840s and lasting well into the twentieth century, minstrel shows popularized the stereotypical images of African Americans. Minstrel troupes first appeared as a formatted style of blackface entertainment in the 1840s. White actors blackened their faces with burnt cork to portray blacks as buffoonish, ignorant characters. Other ethnic minorities, such as Chinese and Irish immigrants, were caricatured, but it was the blackface actors, dancers, musicians, and comedians who captured the fancy of a white America being torn apart by the issue of slavery. Characters such as Jim Crow and Zip Coon built upon the widespread characterizations of Buck, Tom, and Sambo. These minstrels, who marketed themselves as depicting the true culture of African Americans, created debilitating characterizations that remain over a century later. Most of the minstrel originators, however, were white northerners who knew little about African Americans. When in the late 1800s and early 1900s black minstrel troupes became popular, the format and characters were so set it was nearly impossible for black entertainers to break the mold. These black minstrel shows were advertised as presenting "real coons." Yet, ironically, even African Americans had to don burnt cork to represent themselves.[7] Many still-popular songs originated in minstrel shows. "Camptown Races," "My Old Kentucky Home," and "Oh! Susanna," all written by Stephen Foster, tried to capture black Southern life for the northern audience. The fact that Foster never visited the South yet became the most famous minstrel composer illustrates the centrality of stereotype and caricature to the entire project of minstrel shows. In addition to Foster, another northerner, James Bland, enjoyed considerable success as a minstrel actor, then composer. Ironically, Bland, who was black, penned the words to "Carry Me Back to Old Virginny," which became Virginia's state song in 1940. The last stanza captures both the nineteenth-century imagery of the plantation South as well as the popularity of that imagery as late as the twentieth century:

> Carry me back to old Virginny,
> There let me live till I wither and decay,
> Long by the old Dismal Swamp have I wandered,
> There's where this old darkey's life will pass away.
> Massa and missis have long gone before me,
> Soon we will meet on that bright and golden shore,
> There we'll be happy and free from all sorrow,
> There's where we'll meet and we'll never part no more.[8]

Many minstrel songs helped to perpetuate demeaning stereotypes. In 1890, black performer Ernest Hogan wrote a song that featured a young "dusky maiden" who could not choose between two suitors. Ragtime "coon songs" melded black stereotypes and America's newest popular musical genre; in that vein, the song "All Coons Look Alike to Me" became a nationwide sensation. Even respected composers such as George Cohan and Irving Berlin produced songs that perpetuated degenerating stereotypes of African Americans.[9]

By 1909, even though ragtime remained popular, the popularity of minstrel shows was waning. One of the reasons for the death of the minstrel show was the developing technology that brought drama to the big screen. Not surprisingly, the first technological masterpiece in film, *The Birth of a Nation* (1915), celebrated white culture and demeaned African Americans, using many of the same images that were prominent in minstrel shows. Content slaves, lazy freedpeople, and oversexual black men and women dominated the imagery of the film. Most obviously, because none of the prominent characters in the film were portrayed by African American actors, white actors had to don blackface. The movie's producer, D. W. Griffith, enjoyed wide-scale fame for his role in advancing the film industry and in promoting so-called accurate depictions of white and black culture.[10]

But 1916 was also a very different time than the 1840s, particularly in the ability and willingness of African Americans to speak out against such derogatory propaganda like *The Birth of a Nation*. The film's celebration of the Ku Klux Klan as the savior of white Americans prompted the NAACP to protest the movie's release and showing. Though the protests had only limited success in stopping the film's release, they did cause Griffith to cut the most offensive scenes, particularly the castration of an African American man accused of rape.[11] Nonetheless, with the production of *The Birth of Nation,* African American stereotypes found a receptive home in the American media.

In addition to film, another new technology—radio—became an important promoter of black stereotypes. The long-running radio series *Amos 'n' Andy* featured two white actors impersonating contemporary black characters that were direct descendants of Zip Coon and Jim Crow. Some African Americans protested the stereotyping, but the network ignored them and listeners made it a top series for more than a decade. When the series moved to TV in the 1950s, black actors were used—but the spectacle of blacks demeaning themselves had become unsettling, and the show was cancelled in 1953.[12]

In a perverse way, the civil rights movement and the policies it produced in the 1960s helped to ingrain racial stereotypes. The very act by African Americans in calling for government assistance confirmed what opponents of desegregation thought about African Americans—that they were naturally inferior and needed government intervention to lift them up. The old, nineteenth-century stereotypes that minstrel shows helped to perpetuate after the Civil War roared back into fashion. Likewise, the simultaneous white flight from urban centers during the 1960s not only produced huge majorities of African Americans in the nation's largest cities, but also left those municipalities with a rapidly diminishing tax base. Poverty, crime, and family instability—all key components of long-held stereotypes—were rampant in the inner cities and led to the popularization of the term ghetto. Closely associated with African Americans, "the ghetto" became a shorthand, coded reference for stereotypical black problems.

Even in the early twenty-first century, the word *ghetto* evokes powerful imagery and stereotypes. The recently marketed "Ghettopoly" game— a spinoff of Monopoly—uses those stereotypes as its basis. Each of its playing pieces represents either a historical or a modern black stereotype: players choose from a machine gun, a marijuana leaf, a basketball, a 40-ounce beer, or crack cocaine. A recent review of the game highlighted its potent stereotypical imagery:

> According to the instructions, "Da object" of Ghettopoly is "to become the richest playa through stealing, cheating and fencing stolen properties." But the instructions are largely superfluous: you play Ghettopoly exactly as you would Monopoly. Only the terms are different: roll a six, land on Trailer Trash Court, buy it and collect your protection fees ($25, or $120 with a crack house on it). Or roll a two, land on Ghetto Stash and collect $50.[13]

Not surprisingly, critics of the game are numerous. They link it to the long history of stereotypes of, and racism toward, African Americans. Peter Herbert, chair of the Society of Black Lawyers, concluded, "I can't remember seeing anything quite as racist or stereotypical for a long time."[14] Given the length and depth of that history, Herbert's comments are meaningful.

The Rap and Hip-Hop Controversy

"America was born in bling-bling," hip-hop historian Kevin Powell argues. The Founders "had land which was stolen from Native Americans; they owned slaves. So from the very inception of this nation materialism was the order of the day." Powell defends the controversial lyrics and public images of hip-hop artists in his book *Who's Gonna Take the Weight? Manhood, Race and Power in America*. Rather than blame the artists, Powell argues, blame the nation that values crass materialism and that throughout its history has valued black stereotypes.[15]

Since the early 1990s, when an increasing number of African Americans voiced discomfort with fellow black Americans popularizing negative imagery of their culture through rap and hip-hop music, the subject of hip-hop as a social force has been controversial. At its core, hip-hop is nothing more than a very popular modern musical genre. But like all musical forms, hip-hop is rooted in the past. And that past, of course, is not only the rather heroic imagery of oppressed slaves holding onto distinctive West African musical traditions, but also the stereotypical imagery of African Americans as lazy, oversexual, and unintelligent. Thus, as a social and cultural issue, hip-hop stands at the core of the stereotype debate.

Concern among African Americans over rap and hip-hop lyrics is widespread. Instead of facing an onslaught of negative imagery from white people, many black Americans see hip-hop as a kind of cultural treason; African Americans themselves are largely responsible for the production and dissemination of the music, most of which does not cast black people in a positive light. In fact, the music perpetuates the absolute worst imagery of African Americans that dates to the period of enslavement. One notable critic, black pastor Fred Robinson, argues that minstrels "couldn't have done a better job" of promoting stereotypes than some contemporary black artists do. They have "normalized a subculture that is destructive to the well-being of the black community." Even more pointedly, TaRessa Stovall, a journalist who runs the online discussion group "Hip-Hop Degeneration," concludes, "We're glorifying a form of slavery—only it's a form of self-enslavement."[16]

Well-known critic Stanley Crouch, himself African American, decries the stereotyping that other African Americans are responsible for. Crouch argues:

> If one looks at MTV, BET or VH-1 ... the images of black youth are not far removed from those that D.W. Griffith used in *The Birth of a Nation*.... This is the new minstrelsy: the neo-Sambo, mugging or scowling in Trick Daddy's "I'm a Thug," where gold teeth, drop-down pants and tasteless jewelry abound.... These videos are created primarily for the material enrichment of black entertainers, producers and directors, not the present-day whites, who would be run out of the world if they—like the creators of 19th-century minstrelsy—were responsible for the images.[17]

But not everyone agrees that hip-hop artists are to blame. Observers such as Kevin Powell maintain that corporations are not interested in artists who focus on more positive imagery. In 2000, rappers Mos Def and KRS-One challenged the prevailing notion that black artists were to blame. Instead, they claimed, rap and hip-hop were popular because they promoted imagery and ideas about blacks that confirmed whites' thoughts. Chuck D, leader of Public Enemy, has a different take on the matter. "The endorsement of thugs is white people's fantasy of what they want us to be," Chuck D says. Rap and hip-hop are "minstrelsy because that's what white people want to believe about us."[18]

Nonetheless, even musicians considered positive, such as Nas, use lyrics, imagery, and topics that describe, rather than sanitize, street life.[19] So doing may be an accurate representation of reality but also serves to perpetuate stereotypes. For those Americans who believe that a fair amount of reality lurks behind modern stereotypes of African Americans, rap and hip-hop are powerful vehicles for advancing that argument.

FRAMING THE ISSUE

Unlike some of the issues examined in this book, the question of black stereotypes deals considerably less with statistics than it does with abstract issues of perception and propaganda. As such, the stereotypes controversy illustrates that people of different backgrounds can see the same movie or hear the same song and yet have substantially different interpretations of what they saw or heard. Supporters of stereotypes as reality maintain that they would not perpetuate any characterization of an entire group without that representation being based in reality. They argue, for example, that the old minstrel shows grossly mischaracterized African Americans as simpletons. But they also argue that just because those nineteenth-century images were wrong does not mean that modern group characterizations fall into the same trap. To make their point, supporters cite evidence on poverty, children born out of wedlock, and unemployment rates to illustrate that some stereotypes of black people do indeed characterize *some* African Americans accurately.

Opponents, on the other hand, dismiss such statistics, either on their face or as obscuring the real cause for social problems—racism. In fact, many opponents of stereotypes argue that mischaracterization and racism work hand in hand. They contend that Americans will not fully expunge the legacy of slavery and racism completely until they rid popular imagery of black stereotypes and the necessary assumptions that go with them. In short, while opponents of stereotypes recognize that the issue has less immediate significance than criminal punishment, education, or election reform, they see the problem of stereotypes as underlying every African American issue examined in this book.

SUPPORTERS OF STEREOTYPES

Supporters of the argument that stereotypes merely reflect reality base their position on the socioeconomic problems that are particularly prevalent among African Americans. They argue that disproportionately high unemployment, poverty, and imprisonment rates—as well as disproportionately low rates of high school graduation and two-parent families—among African Americans have produced a culture of violence and carelessness. While careful not to project those problems on all black Americans, supporters of the stereotypes-equal-reality position contend that stereotypes merely reflect very real, albeit unfortunate realities for many African Americans. Finally, proponents of this position maintain that the main forces behind the perpetuation of black stereotypes are not white Americans, but black Americans themselves. Obviously, the reality of some rap and hip-hop lyrics do indeed help supporters of this position illustrate that point.

Thomas Sowell

The chief proponent of the position that reality lurks behind black stereotypes is the economist and columnist Thomas Sowell. Derided in some black circles as a modern-day Uncle Tom, Sowell refuses to accept the arguments of some black leaders that stereotypes are not based in reality. He points to a host of statistics that illustrate this point.

In a recent column, Sowell addressed the obvious, but almost taboo, issue of African American players dominating the ranks of professional sports, especially the NBA. Approximately 78 percent of NBA players are African American, and

73 percent of NFL players are black. These statistics have often been central to the debate over stereotypes, as on their face they seem to confirm an important black stereotype that dates to the nineteenth century: African Americans excel at physical activity, such as sports, but not in intellectual activity, such as formal education. While this mindset has certainly fallen out of favor, Sowell argues that it is impossible to deny the reality. He explains:

> Is it just a stereotype that some groups do better at some things than other groups do? Do blacks not really play basketball any better than whites? Do our eyes deceive us when we notice the racial make-up of the NBA? It is one thing to say that everyone should be equal before the law or is entitled to equal opportunity. It is something else to deny the most blatant facts before our eyes, and insist on a dogma of equality of performance, when virtually every individual or group is better at some things than at others.[20]

Thomas Sowell has also questioned the usage of the word *stereotype,* suggesting that complaints about stereotypes merely mask the real problems upon which stereotypes are based. Sowell dismisses "the widespread use of the term 'stereotypes' to dismiss whatever observations or evidence may be cited [about] distinguishing features of particular group behavior patterns."[21] In other words, if the stereotype is actually reality—which Sowell claims is the case for most stereotypes of African Americans—opponents of those perceptions ought to spend more time dealing with the problem rather than blaming those who unfairly perpetuate the stereotype. Sowell asks, "What is the actual reality, as distinguished from 'perceptions' or 'stereotypes?' "[22] When examining statistical evidence on crime, drug use, and poverty—as previous chapters in this book examine—African Americans constitute disproportionately large shares of convicted criminals, drug users, and people living in poverty. Sowell concludes, "Where the implications of a belief can be tested against empirical evidence, then that must be done and the belief rejected if it proves to be inconsistent with the facts . . . But equally, when the empirical evidence reinforces the belief, that too is not to be ignored."[23] If people disagree with explanations for those problems that tend to be based on discrimination and racism, as supporters do, then laying blame for black stereotypes at the feet of black people is the only other option. In the eyes of Thomas Sowell, and certainly for Bill Cosby as well, that is the explanation for the prevalent negative imagery of African Americans.

OPPONENTS OF STEREOTYPES

Opponents of black stereotypes reject them out of hand, arguing that they are modern forms of racism and that they illustrate the nation's continued desire to cast African Americans in a negative light. While critics of stereotypes concede that African Americans do experience disproportionately high poverty, unemployment, and out-of-wedlock births, they point to institutionalized racism—not blacks themselves—as the cause. For opponents, then, the issue of stereotypes goes straight to the heart of the controversies over slave reparations and affirmative action.

Robert Entman and Andrew Rojecki

Both scholars of race in the mass media, Robert Entman and Andrew Rojecki have provided opponents of stereotypes with solid research that validates their position. In their important book *The Black Image in the White Mind,* Entman and Rojecki explore the reality of stereotypes of African Americans by whites. Focusing a considerable amount of attention on representations of blacks in the media, the authors unearth both the history of stereotypes and the underlying cause for their perpetuation: the media. For example, Entman and Rojecki argue,

> The average White mistakenly believes that Blacks constitute one-third of the American population, a majority of the poor, and the bulk of welfare rolls. No wonder, perhaps, so many Whites resentfully overestimate government attention and spending on poverty. Their misimpressions may be reinforced by images—and voids—in the media. Television news tends to illustrate welfare and poverty by portraying urban Blacks rather than the (actually more numerous) rural Whites, furnishing symbolic resources many Whites use to justify resentments.[24]

Fueling an endless cycle of representing misrepresentations, the media, according to Entman and Rojecki, shoulder much of the blame for the continued mischaracterizations of African Americans.

Supporting these claims is a wealth of survey data on whites' views toward African Americans. In a project known as their Indianapolis Study, Entman and Rojecki surveyed white residents of Indianapolis on a host of perceptions of black Americans. Their results show a still-present existence of racial stereotypes. Asked to agree or disagree with a series of statements, respondents exhibited a view of African Americans that corresponds to the stereotypical images of blacks being lazy, impoverished, and prone to commit crime. For example, three-quarters of respondents agreed with the statement that African Americans should overcome racial prejudice on their own, and work "their way up" as Irish, Italians, and Jewish people did. A slightly higher proportion agreed with the statement, "Most Blacks who are on welfare programs could get a job if they really tried." Moreover, about half of the respondents agreed that predominantly black neighborhoods "tend to be run-down" because the residents do not care about their property. Finally, 50 percent of those surveyed saw slavery and historical discrimination as the root causes of black economic stagnation; while this recognizes the significance of those factors, the authors argue, it also shows an acceptance of the stereotype that blacks are economically and socially stagnant.[25]

In addition to portraying African Americans as poor, lazy, and overactive sexually, the media, according to Robert Entman and Andrew Rojecki, constantly hammer home the image of the black criminal. Whereas a white person being murdered is almost always considered newsworthy, the same cannot be said of black murder victims. The authors claim that a murdered African American in a Harlem apartment building "conforms to expectations" created by media images. Consequently, Entman and Rojecki maintain, "Racial representation on television does not appear to match crime statistics, with local news overrepresenting Black perpetrators, underrepresenting Black victims, and overrepresenting White victims." Nationally, the amount of news time devoted to white victims of crime is three times that devoted to black victims. The result is the continued popularity of racial stereotypes.[26]

Perhaps the most subtle yet most undercutting aspect of media representations of African Americans is the type of news stories in which African American commentary is used. A 1997 study of network news programs illustrates that on matters of national or international importance, very few African Americans are used in news stories. For example, in 100 news stories on foreign affairs in 1997, viewers saw 99 sound bites by whites and only one by an African American. Moreover, in 79 news stories on politics, not a single black sound bite was used. But when it came to news stories on sports and discrimination, blacks were overrepresented, serving only to perpetuate the stereotype that African Americans are not learned enough to comment on issues of real significance, and care only about sports and discrimination.[27] Clearly, by quantifying the prevalence of stereotypes, Robert Entman and Andrew Rojecki provide considerable ammunition to the opponents of stereotypes.

Young African Americans Against Media Stereotypes

An increasingly influential voice against stereotypes is the organization Young African Americans Against Media Stereotypes (YAAAMS). The organization focuses on perceptions of blacks in the media, especially those based on African American athletes. In particular, YAAAMS has been concerned with media hype over crimes, or alleged crimes, committed by African American athletes. For example, the organization decries coverage of the 1997 Latrell Sprewell incident, in which the African American NBA player choked his white coach, P. J. Carlesimo. In spite of the media whirlwind surrounding that event, however, YAAAMS contends that there was virtually no coverage of NFL player Kevin Greene, who is white, attacking his coach. Likewise, YAAAMS suggests contrasting the media coverage of Mark Chmura, a white NFL player who was arrested for rape, with the media event of Kobe Bryant's alleged rape of a white woman. Because that image—a black man assaulting a white woman—conforms to the long-standing black stereotype of sexually aggressive African Americans, the media went into a frenzy. In 2004, YAAAMS says, "less than 50 of the 1,500+ pro black athletes (that's 3 percent) got into trouble with the law. But because of the sensationalized, over-hyped coverage of this 3 percent, the media has effectively undermined the image of all professional black athletes."[28]

The organization has also highlighted the problem of how sports commentators perpetuate stereotypes. "Sports commentators have always treated the black athlete differently," the organization claims, "by highlighting the athlete's physical prowess instead of his or her inherent or proven mental abilities, strategies, or training. For example, 'look at his leaping ability' or 'she is very fast' or 'he is such a great athlete.' For the white athlete, 'he is such a hard worker' or 'she plays with her head' or 'what a work ethic.' " Subtle yet powerful references such as these shape public opinion, particularly because they corroborate a conscious or subconscious stereotype of African Americans. Thus, YAAAMS asks, "Is it any wonder that many people believe that black athletes achieve greatness by some fluke of evolution instead of just plain talent and hard work?"[29]

These examples of the competing positions on stereotypes—YAAAMS, Robert Entman and Andrew Rojecki on one side, and Thomas Sowell on the other—illustrate clearly the deep-seated emotions that the issue of black stereotypes evoke. More than a minor cultural issue, stereotypes reflect problems, both within the targeted group, and among those who perpetuate them. Using this issue as an avenue to explore the other issues in this book will not only clarify the question of African American stereotypes, but will also bring into focus nearly every contemporary social and public policy issue relevant to African Americans today.

QUESTIONS AND ACTIVITIES

1. Think about the ethnic and cultural diversity of modern America. What kinds of stereotypes exist of different groups? What prompted the creation and perpetuation of those characterizations?

2. Go to the Project Implicit Web site: https://implicit.harvard.edu/implicit/demo/measureyourattitudes.html. Project Implicit develops online tests that

gauge bias and tendencies toward stereotypes. Take the test. What were the results? Do you have biases that you were not aware of? Compare your test results with those of your classmates, and discuss them.

3. Organize your class into two groups: one that supports the stereotypes-as-reality position and one that opposes stereotypes. Debate the issue, using the arguments from people highlighted in this chapter and evidence from other issues covered in this book. What are the most persuasive points? The most important evidence?

4. Technology has played an important role in the continued presence of black stereotypes. What TV shows, movies, and songs feature negative images of African Americans? Positive images? Does the Internet play as large a role in perpetuating stereotypes as TV and radio?

5. Analyze Bill Cosby's comments about African Americans. Are his words particularly jarring because of his comedy work? Are they more difficult to take seriously given recent allegations that Cosby is guilty of sexual harassment? All in all, do you think that Cosby's comments are helpful or harmful?

NOTES

1. George Curry, "Cosby Wasn't Totally Wrong," *Carolina Peacemaker*, 10–16 June 2004, 6A.

2. Derrick K. Baker, "When Black Folks Condemn Black Folks," *N'DIGO*, 27 May–2 June 2004, 4.

3. DeWayne Wickham, "Cosby Isn't Alone in Asking Blacks to Own Up to Problems," *USA Today*, 25 May 2004.

4. Heather Knight, "Comedian's Call to Action—'Love, Education and Care,'" *San Francisco Chronicle*, 10 December 2004.

5. Stanley M. Elkins, *Slavery: A Problem in American Institutional and Intellectual Life* (Chicago: University of Chicago Press, 1976 [1959]), 82–89.

6. Dora Apel, *Imagery of Lynching: Black Men, White Women, and the Mob* (London: Rutgers University Press, 2004).

7. W. T. Lahmon Jr., *Raising Cain: Blackface Performance from Jim Crow to Hip Hop* (Cambridge, Mass.: Harvard University Press, 2000).

8. James Bland, "Carry Me Back to Old Virginny," 1873. Given the offensive nature of the lyrics, in 1997 the Virginia legislature gave the song emeritus status and began searching for a replacement.

9. Edward A. Berlin, *Ragtime: A Musical and Cultural History* (Berkeley: University of California Press, 1980).

10. "The Birth of a Nation," Film Site, http://www.filmsite.org/birt.html.

11. "Today in History: February 8, 1915," Library of Congress American Memory Web site, http://memory.loc.gov/ammem/today/feb08.html.

12. Donald Bogle, *Toms, Coons, Mulattoes, Mammies and Bucks: An Interpretive History of Blacks in American Films* (New York: Continuum Books, 2000), 72, 102, 107.

13. Tim Dowling, "I Rolled a Two—and Got a Ghetto Stash," *Guardian*, 21 January 2004.

14. Ibid.

15. John Blake, "25 Years of Hip-Hop," *Atlanta Journal-Constitution,* 30 September 2004.

16. Ibid.

17. Stanley Crouch, "A Lost Generation and Its Exploiters," *New York Times,* 26 August 2001.

18. Allison Samuels, N'Gai Croal, and David Gates; with Alisha Davis, "Battle for the Soul of Hip-Hop," *Newsweek,* 9 October 2000, 58.

19. Jim Farber, "The World According to Nas," *New York Daily News,* 28 November 2004.

20. Thomas Sowell, "Stereotypes about Stereotypes," 17 March 2002, Townhall Online Magazine, http://www.townhall.com/columnists/thomassowell/ts20020517.shtml.

21. Thomas Sowell, *Race and Culture: A World View* (New York: Basic Books, 1994), 11.

22. Ibid., 110.

23. Ibid., 13.

24. Robert M. Entman and Andrew Rojecki, *The Black Image in the White Mind* (Chicago: University of Chicago Press, 2000), 8–9.

25. Ibid., 22–26.

26. Ibid., 81.

27. Ibid., 62–65.

28. http://www.yaaams.com/blackathletes.shtml.

29. Ibid.

SUGGESTED READING

Apel, Dora. *Imagery of Lynching: Black Men, White Women, and the Mob.* London: Rutgers University Press, 2004.

Baker, Derrick K. "When Black Folks Condemn Black Folks." *N'DIGO,* 27 May–2 June 2004, p. 4.

Berlin, Edward A. *Ragtime: A Musical and Cultural History.* Berkeley: University of California Press, 1980.

Blake, John. "25 Years of Hip-Hop." *Atlanta Journal-Constitution,* 30 September 2004.

Bogle, Donald. *Toms, Coons, Mulattoes, Mammies and Bucks: An Interpretive History of Blacks in American Films.* New York: Continuum Books, 2000.

Crouch, Stanley. "A Lost Generation and Its Exploiters." *New York Times,* 26 August 2001.

Curry, George. "Cosby Wasn't Totally Wrong." *Carolina Peacemaker,* 10–16 June 2004, p. 6A.

Dates, Jannette L., and William Barlow, eds. *Split Image: African Americans in the Mass Media.* Washington, D.C.: Howard University Press, 1993.

Dowling, Tim. "I Rolled a Two—and Got a Ghetto Stash." *Guardian,* 21 January 2004.

Elkins, Stanley M. *Slavery: A Problem in American Institutional and Intellectual Life.* Chicago: University of Chicago Press, 1976 [1959].

Entman, Robert M., and Andrew Rojecki. *The Black Image in the White Mind*. Chicago: University of Chicago Press, 2000.

Farber, Jim. "The World According to Nas." *New York Daily News*, 28 November 2004.

Hoberman, John. *Darwin's Athletes: How Sport Has Damaged Black America and Preserved the Myth of Race*. New York: Houghton Mifflin, 1997.

Knight, Heather. "Comedian's Call to Action—'Love, Education and Care.'" *San Francisco Chronicle*, 10 December 2004.

Lahmon, W. T., Jr. *Raising Cain: Blackface Performance from Jim Crow to Hip Hop*. Cambridge: Harvard University Press, 2000.

Samuels, Allison, N'Gai Croal, and David Gates. "Battle for the Soul of Hip-Hop." *Newsweek*, 9 October 2000, p. 58.

Sowell, Thomas. *Race and Culture: A World View*. New York: BasicBooks, 1994.

———. "Stereotypes about Stereotypes." *Townhall Online Magazine*, 17 March 2002, http://www.townhall.com/columnists/thomassowell/ts20020517.shtml.

Wickham, DeWayne. "Cosby Isn't Alone in Asking Blacks to Own Up to Problems." *USA Today*, 25 May 2004.

Videos

Goodtimes Home Video. *Amos N' Andy: Anatomy of a Controversy*. 60 min. 1997.

Reid, Francis. *Skin Deep*. 53 min. 1995. Traces the racial bias of several college students. California Newsreel, http://www.newsreel.org.

Riggs, Marlon. *Black Is ... Black Ain't*. 87 min. 1995. Examines stereotypes, identity, and "blackness" of African Americans. California Newsreel, http://www.newsreel.org.

Riggs, Marlon. *Ethnic Notions*. 56 minutes. 1987. "Traces the evolution of the deeply rooted stereotypes which have fueled anti-Black prejudice. Loyal Toms, carefree Sambos, faithful mammies, ridiculous coons and wide-eyed pickaninnies permeated popular culture from the antebellum period to the civil rights era, planting themselves deep in the American psyche." California Newsreel, http://www.newsreel.org.

Web Sites

Project Implicit, https://implicit.harvard.edu/implicit/demo/measureyourattitudes.html.

Tolerance.org Web site, http://www.tolerance.org.

Young African Americans Against Stereotypes, http//:www.yaaams.com.

9

ELECTION REFORM

On November 3, 2000, Americans woke up expecting the drawn-out presidential campaign to be over. Either Vice President Al Gore or Governor George W. Bush had won, or so they thought. But upon turning on the morning news, Americans witnessed an unthinkable event in the technology age: the winner of the election could not be determined. In fact, the day after voting was merely the beginning of a 36-day drama between the Gore and Bush camps, each accusing the other of interfering with the counting of votes. "Hanging chads" and "butterfly ballots" became the buzzwords of the moment as election workers in Florida attempted to ascertain the winner of that state's 25 electoral votes. A key part of that process was the attempt to ensure that voting rights—particularly those of African Americans—were being protected.

Consequently, African Americans found themselves once again at the center of national controversy. That 9 of every 10 black voters favored Al Gore infused the controversy with partisan bickering and even worse—accusations of fraud and the denial of suffrage. The eventual outcome of the election, George W. Bush's victory, confirmed for many African Americans their sense that all of the legal wrangling and political posturing was explicitly designed to disenfranchise them. While plenty of people, including some African Americans, disagreed with that analysis, the nation's history of poll taxes, literacy tests, grandfather clauses, and other obstacles to black suffrage meant that even spurious accusations deserved attention. The result, even several years after the election of 2000, has been a renewed focus on election reform, which is the subject of this chapter.

Supporters of election reform point to the election of 2000 and, to a lesser extent, the election of 2004 as evidence of the need for reform. At the root of their calls for change is the belief that African Americans have been disenfranchised. Supporters claim that registration procedures place unnecessary obstacles in the voting process and provide a means to intimidate minority voters. Opponents dismiss those concerns out of hand and argue that, if reform is needed, it should strengthen, not weaken, laws that allow voter registration without identification. By examining the primary arguments of each position and highlighting the major figures on each side, this chapter demonstrates that, in many ways, the issue of election reform encapsulates every other African American issue covered in this book.

Election of 2000

In early November 2000, as the Bush and Gore campaigns pushed their legal teams into high gear, few Americans could have predicted the topsy-turvy events that would leave the election hanging in the balance. Just as voters were learning of the razor-thin margin between the candidates, the real problem began to surface: allegations of voting irregularities in Palm Beach County, Florida. Contending that their punch-card ballots were configured in a confusing manner, many voters in Palm Beach suggested that the butterfly design was intentional. In the overwhelmingly Democratic county, dozens of voters said that their intended vote for Vice President Gore might actually have been cast for third-party candidate Pat Buchanan. As election board workers prepared for the required recount (because the margin was less than 0.5% of total votes cast), growing concerns over irregularities began to dominate the media coverage in Florida.

As the drama unfolded, African American voters in Florida found themselves at center stage. Had the election controversy emerged in another state—particularly one without a sizable black population—the 2000 election and its aftermath might have had little to do with African Americans. But the fact that Florida does have a significant African American population (15%), and that, as a southern state, its segregationist past is well known, made the 2000 election controversy a microcosm of the struggle for black voting rights. Moreover, as the Gore campaign identified the four counties for which manual recounts would be necessary, the centrality of black Americans to the election saga was cemented. Palm Beach (14% African American), Volusia (10%), Palm Beach (20%) and Broward (20%) each had significant numbers of black voters. Because Gore enjoyed the support of more than

90 percent of African Americans nationwide, his and their plight rested in the hands of those manually recounting the ballots.[1]

This fact was not lost on African American leaders. Just after the Bush campaign sued to stop the manual recount in those four counties, black advocacy groups coalesced around the Gore camp's push to maintain the recounts. That Bush's legal team used the equal protection clause of the 14th Amendment to argue for stopping the recounts galvanized those groups even more. Moreover, even though George Bush's brother, Florida governor Jeb Bush, had recused himself from the legal fight, Florida's Republican secretary of state, Katherine Harris, became the main object of black voters' frustrations. A precinct-by-precinct analysis by the *Washington Post* found that the higher the percentage of black voters in a district, the higher the rate of rejected ballots.[2] Armed with such evidence, African Americans began lobbying furiously for a full statewide recount. Reverend Jesse Jackson concluded, "About 80 percent of the voters who were disenfranchised were African-Americans. If you forget to vote, you feel guilty. If you vote, and your vote is taken away, you feel angry."[3]

That anger became fury when, on December 12, the U.S. Supreme Court ruled that the manual recount could not continue. The majority of justices determined that the equal protection clause of the 14th Amendment prevented the different handling of different voters' ballots; the recount, as well as the determination of a voter's intent by county canvassing boards examining ballots with hanging and dimpled chads, was an affront to this clause, argued the majority.[4] Controversial among voters and controversial among legal scholars, *Bush v. Gore* effectively ended the election. The next night, Al Gore conceded, but many supporters—especially African Americans—vowed electoral revenge. Not only would they punish Republican candidates at the polls in 2002 and 2004, they would also agitate for a major overhaul of the nation's election system.

In fact, as the 2000 election drama came to a close, African American voters and political leaders laid the groundwork for that reform. Just days after the Supreme Court decision, Jesse Jackson declared, "Florida is the scene of the crime. It's what Birmingham and Selma was. This is where the state legislators seek to overthrow the people's election. This is where Jeb Bush and Katherine Harris organized the state to target African-Americans."[5] Barnstorming the country to highlight the alleged electoral abuses of African American voters, Jackson and many African American leaders called for a week of "moral outrage and indignation." Only through such action, Jackson argued, would the disenfranchisement of black voters finally end.[6]

As the angst among black Americans over the election intensified, many called for their elected leaders to take action. The Congressional Black Caucus took the lead, calling for a thorough investigation and for sweeping reforms of the nation's electoral system. In March 2001, the caucus held public hearings aimed at raising awareness of the problem. Prominent black leaders such as NAACP president Kweisi Mfume, testified. Mfume argued that the focus on the election aftermath obscured problems that his organization had seen coming in the weeks before election day. "We were appalled and outraged by much of what we saw the weekend before the election," Mfume said, charging that these actions occurred "at polling places on election day and at boards of elections throughout Florida in the days and weeks that followed." By focusing on questionable events that occurred prior to the election, the testimony succeeded in expanding the areas of concern. Subsequent recommendations included the retraining of election workers, the modernization of voting machines, the establishment of clear standards for bilingual ballots, and the launch of an aggressive voter education initiative. Seeing dimpled chads and butterfly ballots as the least of their worries, the Congressional Black Caucus portrayed the election irregularities as being the most recent example in a history of voter intimidation.[7] By connecting the election to the history of black suffrage in America, the leaders of the Congressional Black Caucus were making a potent—and politically explosive—argument.

HISTORICAL CONTEXT

The history of African Americans agitating for voting rights is long, mainly because each success seemed to be met with disappointment. Therefore, the history of African Americans actually voting is short. Just as supporters of election reform point to the checkered past of the nation's voting laws, that past includes several phases in which black Americans were disenfranchised. A brief look at that history will help place the current issue of election reform in context.

As discussed in reference to the 2000 election, the Constitution says nothing about voting qualifications; determining those qualifications was the domain of states until the passage of the 15th Amendment (1870), which granted African Americans suffrage. The result, from period to period, has been that different generations set the requirements for suffrage. Not surprisingly, then, the eighteenth and nineteenth centuries constituted a period of little hope for black Americans wanting to vote. In most states, not even free blacks—who, like whites, paid taxes, served in militias, and were landowners—could vote. Thus, when the Civil War began in 1861, African Americans in both the North and South hoped that the Lincoln administration would steadily alter the war's goals from merely preserving the Union to include ending slavery and pushing for something resembling equal rights among blacks and whites. By the time the war ended in 1865, African Americans had gotten their wish regarding slavery; the issue of equal rights, including voting, lay in the hands of a small but influential minority of radical Republican congressmen.[8]

Those radical Republicans succeeded in pushing for African American voting rights. Following the Civil Rights Act of 1866, the 14th Amendment was ratified in 1868 to provide citizenship to African Americans. Former Confederate states' terms for readmission, as dictated by the radicals, included ratification of that amendment. The next step was tackling voting rights. The 15th Amendment gave the new citizens the right to vote. Nonetheless, the right of African Americans to vote and hold office was challenged from the very beginning. Southern states took advantage of ambiguities in the amendment to limit dramatically the number of blacks who could vote. Poll taxes, literacy tests, grandfather clauses—as well as outright intimidation—became common obstacles for African Americans wanting to exercise suffrage. Congress responded by trying to eliminate the most significant organization opposed to black voting, the Ku Klux Klan, but in reality had little success. The Confederacy may have lost the war, but it had won the political issue over states' rights.[9]

Enforcement of the Reconstruction Act provided blacks with a majority of the vote in most Southern states. Between 1870 and 1900, 22 African Americans served in Congress. In 1868, Louisiana elected a black lieutenant governor, Oscar Dunn. African Americans outnumbered whites in the South Carolina legislature by 87 to 40. The Reconstruction-era representation of African Americans was short-lived, however. In 1876, after three years of controversy, the U.S. Senate refused to seat P.B.S. Pinchback, an African American from Louisiana who had been elected in 1873. Also in 1876, the Supreme Court began to back away from African American voting rights, ruling that "the right of suffrage is not a necessary attribute of national citizenship."[10] Ironically, later that year, disputed election returns from three states—Louisiana, South Carolina, and Florida—threw the outcome of the presidential election into question. After months of wrangling, the election was decided when the Democratic candidate, Samuel J. Tilden, gave up his fight in exchange for the victorious candidate, Republican Rutherford B. Hayes, ending Reconstruction upon taking office. Whatever promise the 15th Amendment gave African Americans, it evaporated with the withdrawal of federal troops and authority in 1877.

The end of Reconstruction allowed for the full-fledged onset of Redemption, by which white southerners opposed to blacks voting unleashed a relentless intimidation campaign. In 1878, the U.S. attorney general revealed widespread intimidation of African Americans attempting to vote and stuffing of the ballot boxes in several states. In Georgia, African American state representatives were expelled from their seats because of their race. The success of whites in stamping out African American suffrage led to the emergence of Jim Crow, a comprehensive regime of intimidation and violence that was not ended until the 1960s.[11]

By 1890, Mississippi had inaugurated the first of the constitutional conventions that would sweep the South and begin the systematic exclusion of African Americans from the political arena. By 1896, voting rights for African Americans triggered riots across the South, and Representative George White of North Carolina became the only African American remaining in the Congress. Between 1896 and 1900 the number of black voters in Louisiana was reduced from 130,000 to 5,000. Obviously, in spite of the 15th Amendment, black voters could not overcome the onslaught of Redemption without the help of the federal government.

In the 1960s, that onslaught began to abate as the civil rights movement reached a critical mass. In 1964, two-thirds of the states adopted the 24th Amendment of the U.S. Constitution, which prohibited states from denying citizens the right to vote by the use of a poll tax. Within months after Bloody Sunday in Selma, Alabama, President Lyndon Johnson signed into law the Voting Rights Act of 1965.[12] Black voter registration in southern states skyrocketed: from 1960 to 1966, Mississippi witnessed a 700 percent increase, Alabama a 300 percent increase, and South Carolina a 200 percent increase in the number of African Americans registered to vote. In the 1970s and 1980s, however, in response to continued violations of the Voting Rights Act, Congress renewed and strengthened the law. In short, what had begun nearly a century earlier—efforts to extend black men suffrage by the radical Republicans—was finally cemented in 1965.

Since the 1960s, both black voter registration and the number of black elected officials have increased dramatically. By 2000, nearly two-thirds of all eligible African Americans had registered to vote. Moreover, between 1972 and 1992, the number of African Americans in Congress from the South increased from 0 to 17. Likewise, the overall number of black elected officials in the South went from 1,179 in 1973 to 4,924 in 1993. Understanding the long struggle for black voting rights, as well as the relatively recent progress in registration and election of African Americans, provides a helpful context for appreciating the level of concern for national election reform.

National Commission on Federal Election Reform

Thus, while the Congressional Black Caucus and African American leaders such as Jesse Jackson took the grassroots lead in promoting election reform,

Congress took a major step. In January 2001, Congress created the National Commission on Federal Election Reform, which was charged with "assuring pride and confidence in the electoral process." The commission's bipartisan composition was highlighted by its principal cochairs, former presidents Gerald Ford and Jimmy Carter. After holding four public meetings at different sites across the country, and after numerous hearings, the commission submitted its final recommendations for reform. Those recommendations have become the foundation for subsequent calls for election reform.

The commission's recommendations, outlined in table 9.1, themselves became controversial. Decried as focusing too much on machinery, the commission's proposals did little to allay concerns by African American voters regarding voter intimidation. William Raspberry, a well-known African American columnist, declared that, after months of labor, all the commission produced was

Table 9.1   The Thirteen Policy Recommendations of the National Commission on Federal Election Reform

1. Every state should adopt a system of statewide voter registration.
2. Every state should permit provisional voting.
3. Presidential and congressional elections should be held on a national holiday.
4. Congress should simplify absentee voting by military and overseas citizens.
5. Every state should restore voting rights to convicted felons who have fully served their sentence.
6. The state and federal governments should take additional steps to ensure the voting rights of all citizens, and should enforce the principle of one person, one vote.
7. Every state should set a benchmark for voting system performance.
8. The federal government should develop a comprehensive set of voting equipment standards.
9. States should adopt uniform statewide standards for defining what will constitute a vote on each type of voting machine.
10. News organizations should not project any presidential election results in any state while polls remain open elsewhere.
11. The federal government should provide matching funds to states in order to modernize election systems.
12. A new federal agency, the Election Administration Commission, should be created to oversee the federal responsibilities proposed by this commission.
13. Congress should enact legislation that includes federal assistance for election administration.

Source: National Commission on Federal Election Reform, *To Assure Pride and Confidence in the Electoral Process* (August 2001), http://www.tcf.org/Publications/ElectionReform/99_full_report.pdf.

"a mouse of a report."[13] One critic could barely maintain a modicum of civility in his analysis: "Bipartisan reform commissions usually pair Democratic con men with Republican chumps. The National Commission on Federal Election Reform (ex-Presidents Jimmy Carter and Gerald Ford honorary co-chairs) was no exception."[14] In light of the public's lukewarm response to the commission's proposals, Congress had its work cut out for itself as it attempted to tackle the issue of election reform.

Help America Vote Act

The practical problem created by the commission's proposals was that little momentum had been established for a reform agenda to which both sides could agree. As Congress took up, and eventually took action on, the issue, its own response left too many issues unanswered. The result was the Help America Vote Act (HAVA), which became law in 2002. The Help America Vote Act created national standards for the administration of all federal, state, and local elections. More than $3.8 billion was earmarked for improvements in voting technology and the election process. Though Congress did not incorporate every proposal of the reform commission, some of those suggestions were incorporated into the law.

HAVA impacts every part of the voting process, from voting machines to provisional ballots, from voter registration to poll worker training. Election officials, legislators, and advocates in each state are responsible for implementing HAVA properly. Under HAVA, states must meet many new federal requirements. They will have to issue provisional ballots, create statewide computerized voter lists, allow for second-chance voting, and increase access for disabled voters. States have received federal funds for these purposes and for improving the administration of elections. To be eligible for such funds, however, each state had to design a plan, pass enabling legislation, and devote a small amount of state funds to HAVA implementation. Each state also had to develop a phase of citizen participation and public review.

For supporters of reform, HAVA represented a step in the right direction. But they saw it only as that: a step. Opponents, on the other hand, saw HAVA as a sufficient response to the problems highlighted by the 2000 election. As both sides prepared for the election of 2004, each found in it evidence for its side. While the outcome of the election was delayed two days because of recounts in Ohio, the election controversy did not reach anything approaching the level of crisis of 2000. Nonetheless, with ballot security questions as well as provisional ballot legitimacy questions, the election of 2004 did add fuel to the fire of election reform. An examination of each side's major arguments will help to frame the issue.

FRAMING THE ISSUE

In addition to assessing whether HAVA needs to be altered, both support-ers and opponents of election reform have their eyes on another opportunity to advocate their ideas: the reauthorization of key components of the Voting Rights Act in 2007. Thus, even though much of the debate over election reform seems framed by the past—for example, the 2000 and 2004 elections, the proposals of the election reform commission, and HAVA—neither side is satisfied with the state of affairs in national elections.

Supporters of reform argue that HAVA did not go far enough in three key areas of concern: uniform voting machinery, ease of registration, and banning states from rendering convicted felons ineligible to vote. Propo-nents maintain that without each state using the same kind of machinery, opportunities for human error or worse—fraud—abound. Given the long history of black disenfranchisement in the United States, supporters are particularly concerned that until the federal government dedicates more money to the purchasing of uniform voting machinery, the government cannot guarantee the principle of one person, one vote. Likewise, reform supporters argue that the federal government must dedicate far more resources than it already does to streamline voter registration, not to men-tion attracting more potential voters through get-out-the-vote campaigns. Perceiving deadlines and paperwork in the registration process as modern-day poll taxes and literacy tests, reform proponents suggest that unregis-tered voters ought to be able to register and vote on election day. Finally, supporters argue that convicted felons who have completed their sentence must be allowed to vote, and the federal government must prevent states from declaring such people ineligible.

Opponents of reform chafe at the dramatically increased role of the fed-eral government in the proposals of reform supporters. Though many oppo-nents would concede that some election reforms must be made—especially updated voting technology and the security of the voting and recounting processes—they do not agree that this is a federal power. Thus, seeing elec-tion reform as an issue of federal versus states' rights, opponents support the rights of states to determine which technology they use, registration deadlines and requirements, and whether felons in their jurisdiction ought to have the right to vote. Moreover, opponents argue that if any reform should happen at the federal level, that should be the repeal of the National Voter Registra-tion Act of 1993 (commonly known as the Motor Voter Law), which allows people to register to vote in driver's licensing offices. Opponents suggest that the watered-down requirements for identification—as required by Motor Voter—have invited considerable fraud that surfaced in 2000 and 2004.

SUPPORTERS OF REFORM

Proponents of election reform contend that fair and open elections in the United States have been obstructed by a series of maladies that HAVA did not address satisfactorily: antiquated voting machines that fail to accurately record voters' choices; ballots that confuse rather than clarify; overcrowded polling places; polling places that are inaccessible to the disabled, to the blind, and to non–English speakers; inaccurate voter registration lists; and so-called ballot security measures that have the effect, if not the intent, of intimidating and discouraging voters. Consequently, supporters argue, HAVA must be expanded, which necessarily involves the federal government enlarging its oversight and authority over the election process.

The Advancement Project

Perhaps the most influential organization among those that support election reform is the Advancement Project. A racial justice group that usually employs legal action to achieve its goals, the Advancement Project saw its membership and visibility skyrocket following the 2000 election controversy.

Judith A. Browne, acting director of the Advancement Project, focused the organization's efforts on the 2004 election. While most Americans concluded that the 2004 election was much smoother than the previous one, Browne completely disagrees. Pointing to alleged irregularities in Ohio and Florida in 2004, Browne argues that this continued evidence of voter intimidation through challenging voter credentials has a direct link to the nation's long history of disenfranchising black voters:

> A review of the history of challenge statutes in Florida and Ohio demonstrates that those laws are rooted in this country's sordid history of racial oppression. The Florida challenge statute, for example, was passed in 1868, just one year after Blacks were granted the right to vote in Florida.... The Ohio statute, originally codified in 1831, was amended in 1859 to permit challenges based upon a voter's possession of a "visible admixture of African blood." In 1868, the law was again amended to include questions for challenged voters about their racial identity and the racial composition of their neighborhoods and schools. In 2004, there was serious concern that the discriminatory nature of these statutes would be resurrected.[15]

As Browne's statement indicates, her organization is focused less on voting machinery and more on continued oppression of black voters. In addition to voter intimidation generally, the group has focused on changing laws in states that bar convicted felons from voting. Virginia takes away certain civil rights, including the right to vote, from any individual convicted of a felony.

"Formerly incarcerated people are unjustly shut out of our democracy based on a history of racial discrimination and administrative confusion," says Edward Hailes Jr., the Advancement Project's senior attorney. The group laments that the United States is the only democracy that indefinitely bars former felons from voting. To make its point, Advancement Project claims that 4.6 million Americans—or 1 in 50 adults—have been deprived of the right to vote as a result of felony convictions. Nearly three-quarters of those disenfranchised by felon laws are no longer in prison. Moreover, because a disproportionately high number of African Americans are imprisoned (as discussed in chapter 5), this issue hits African American voters particularly hard. For example, in Virginia, 1 in 4 African American men (110,000) cannot vote because of that state's law regarding convicted felons' voting rights.[16]

Mary Frances Berry

As former chairwoman of the U.S. Commission on Civil Rights, Mary Frances Berry took a leading role in pushing for election reform after the 2000 debacle. After holding hearings that were separate from those convened by the National Commission on Federal Election Reform, Berry's agency issued its own report. Pointing to new voting laws passed by the Florida legislature and supported by Governor Jeb Bush, Berry remarked, "The election-reform measures signed into law by Gov. Jeb Bush have the potential to rectify many of the problems noted in our report. However, there are significant concerns that were not addressed by the legislation. We want to get a sense of what's working, what's not, and what more can be done."[17]

Mary Frances Berry's efforts to raise awareness of the potential problems in Florida were successful. Mainstream media outlets soon turned their own antennae to the areas of the state in which serious problems were alleged. Perhaps the most notorious was Gadsden County. With three-fifths of its population African Americans, Gadsden seemed to be a natural place to turn for those searching for possible race-based voting irregularities. What Berry and journalists found was startling: the county's voting machines had failed to count the ballots of 2,085 voters. Given the likelihood that the majority of these voters cast their ballots for Al Gore, supporters of reform concluded that these voters were "technologically disenfranchised." Though Berry's actions on this matter did not result in Gadsden County's problems reaching the national spotlight, the still-existent frustration over the situation in 2000 has kept the fire for reform alive.[18]

By agitating for additional action, Berry became a lightning rod of controversy, which culminated in President Bush not renewing her term on the Civil Rights Commission. Nevertheless, Berry remains an icon of the election reform movement, if for no other reason than her own childhood experiences with segregation and disenfranchisement. A personification of the struggle for black civil rights, Berry continues to push for the kind of radical election reform that causes opponents to be alarmed.

OPPONENTS OF REFORM

Those opposed to election reform are not oblivious to what happened in 2000. In fact, many of them have urged state legislatures to ensure the integrity of the registration, voting, and recounting processes. Opponents' central rub with reform supporters, therefore, is over which entity—the federal government or state governments—ought to have control over such questions. Moreover, reform opponents argue that many of the claims made by supporters—particularly those involving allegations of race-based irregularities—are exaggerated, and perhaps completely imagined. If any reform should occur, opponents argue, state and federal governments ought to ensure that voter registration rolls are kept current, that voting technology is maintained, and that the process for recounts is clear and ironclad.

The Cato Institute

As the nation's leading libertarian think tank, the Cato Institute was, and is, adamantly opposed to any election reforms that give more power to the federal government. Cato's central argument against such change is a strict interpretation of the Constitution that precludes Congress from overriding state and local voting laws except in extraordinary cases. Contending that the 2000 election was not extraordinary, Cato has urged Congress not to react to the political pressure supporting election reform. "Congress should preserve the primacy of the states in electoral administration," Cato's researchers argue. "If Congress decides to spend federal tax money on elections, the funds should go to the states without any strings attached. Nationalizing elections through federal mandates would be a constitutional and policy mistake."[19]

As for ballot problems, Cato argues that voters are responsible for casting a ballot properly. So-called assistance by election workers only invites fraud, argues the organization. Just as voters are responsible for educating themselves about the candidates and the issues in an election, they must be held solely accountable for the ballots they cast. Even the ambitious voter-registration drives pose problems, the group claims, because individual citizens—without prodding or persuasion—should decide for themselves if they want to be registered to vote. As the election of 2004 illustrated, even the massive registration and get-out-the-vote drives did little to increase voter turnout.

Cato's biggest concern is the role of the federal government. Arguing that the states should be free to make their own decisions about voting equipment and voter registration systems, the group contends that states should consider sharply limiting absentee and other voting outside the polling place. Provisional voting, which caused most of the problems in Ohio in 2004, has proven to be costly both in money and in time. In short, the federal government's role in reforming the election process should be limited, and states must determine for themselves how to prevent another Florida-like debacle from occurring.

Todd Gaziano

The director for legal and judicial studies at the Heritage Foundation, Todd Gaziano became a leading opponent of calls for federal-based election reform. Gaziano agreed with reform supporters that many problems with registration, voting, and recounting occurred, but disagreed vehemently that these problems stemmed from intimidation of minority voters and from policies that effectively disenfranchised voters. Rather, Gazanio argues, the problems that surfaced in 2000 were the result of the most important election law passed by Congress since the Voting Rights Act: the Motor Voter Law of 1993. Gaziano concludes that Motor Voter, not the alleged culprits mentioned by reform advocates, is the main cause for concern.

In testimony to Congress, Gaziano highlighted problems created by the law, which he says

> has helped create the most inaccurate voting rolls in our history. Citizens are registered in multiple jurisdictions at the same time, and very few states have effective procedures to ensure that those registered even are citizens. If you compound our sloppy voting rolls with the fact that over 15 percent of Wisconsin college students in one survey admitted voting more than once (several voted at least five times) and that absentee voter fraud has plagued many recent contests, you can almost guarantee that illegal voting may provide the margin of victory in a close contest. The most technically advanced nation and leader of the free world should do a better job of policing its democratic processes.[20]

In short, Gaziano argues, the allegations by reform supporters are not only incorrect, but also get in the way of effectively handling problems in the nation's elections. Calling measures that are designed to ensure ballot security and the integrity of voting rolls "disenfranchisement" may be politically popular in some circles, he argues, but does little to correct those problems.

Clearly, then, little common ground exists between Americans who support and Americans who oppose election reforms. Likely the result of generations of political posturing, this controversy is also the result of generations of unquestionable disenfranchisement of African Americans. Until more distance is placed between that history and today, the issue of election reform will not become any less explosive.

QUESTIONS AND ACTIVITIES

1. Organize your class into two groups. One group will adopt the position of election reform supporters, while the other will adopt the position of reform opponents. Begin a debate of the issue. Which points are most persuasive? Are there arguments that are based more on emotion or political appeal rather than substance or fact?

2. Research the voter registration, provisional ballot, and recounting laws in your state. Given what you have read in this chapter, are these laws effective in maintaining the integrity of elections in your state?

3. Research examples of alleged voter fraud. As a class, discuss the most impressive example of fraud that each of you has read about. What kinds of laws would be needed to ensure that those actions do not happen? Would they be more effective as federal laws or state laws?

4. Interview family members, friends, or neighbors who are 65 years or older. Ask them for their perspective on election reform. Do they think the federal government should be involved? Do they believe that much of the allegations of fraud are true? Have they seen any changes in their lifetime in how voters have been treated? Report back to your classmates, highlighting the most significant things you learned from the interviews.

NOTES

1. For an excellent timeline of key events in the election and its aftermath, see National Public Radio's Election 2000 Web site, http://www.npr.org/news/national/election2000/#.

2. John Mintz and Dan Keating, "Florida Ballot Spoilage Likelier for Blacks; Voting Machines, Confusion Cited," *Washington Post,* 3 December 2000.

3. Julie Hauserman, "Jesse Jackson: Florida 'is the Scene of the Crime,'" *St. Petersburg Times,* 14 December 2000, B5.

4. "The 43rd President; Text of Supreme Court Ruling in *Bush v. Gore* Florida Recount Case," *New York Times,* 14 December 2000.

5. Hauserman, "Jesse Jackson."

6. C. Lori Peréz, "The 2000 Presidential Election, Postelection Contest: A Chronology," *Journal of American History* Web site, http://www.indiana.edu/~jah/election2000/.

7. "Black Caucus Holds Special Election Reform Hearing on Capitol Hill," *Jet,* March 19, 2001, 12.

8. Alexander Keyssar, *The Right to Vote: The Contested History of Democracy in the United States* (New York: Basic Books, 2000), 87–104.

9. Ibid., 104–16.

10. *U.S. v. Crukshank,* 92 U.S. 542 (1876).

11. Eric Foner, *Reconstruction: America's Unfinished Revolution* (New York: HarperCollins, 1988), 564–87.

12. Keyssar, *Right to Vote,* 263–69.

13. William Raspberry, "A Major Waste of Opportunity," *Denver Post,* 3 August 2001.

14. Don Feder, "Election Panels 'Fixes' a Disaster," *Boston Globe,* 8 August 2001.

15. Statement of Judith A. Browne, "Voting in 2004: Report to the Nation on America's Election Process," The Advancement Project Web site, 7 December 2004, http://www.advancementproject.org/reptonat.pdf.

16. "Updated Virginia Handbook to Help Formerly Incarcerated People Restore Their Voting Rights," Power and Democracy Web site, The Advancement Project, http://www.advancementproject.org/power.html.

17. Bill Cotterell, "Election Reforms Get More Review," *Tallahassee Democrat,* 10 June 2002.

18. Walton Hanes, "The Disenfranchisement of the African American Voter in the 2000 Presidential Election: The Silence of the Winner and Loser," *Black Scholar* 31 (2002): 21–24.

19. John Samples, "Election Reform, Federalism, and the Obligation of Voters," Cato Institute Web site, 23 October 2001, http://www.cato.org/pub_display.php?pub_id=1276.

20. Testimony of Todd F. Gaziano to Congress, 14 March 2001, http://www.heritage.org/Research/GovernmentReform/Test031401.cfm.

SUGGESTED READING

Ackerman, Bruce, ed. *Bush v. Gore: The Question of Legitimacy.* New Haven: Yale University Press, 2002.

"Black Caucus Holds Special Election Reform Hearing on Capitol Hill." *Jet,* 19 March 2001.

Browne, Judith A., statement of. "Voting in 2004: Report to the Nation on America's Election Process." The Advancement Project Web site, 7 December 2004, http://www.advancementproject.org/reptonat.pdf.

Cotterell, Bill. "Election Reforms Get More Review." *Tallahassee Democrat,* 10 June 2002.

Crigler, Ann N., Marion R. Just, and Edward J. McCaffery, eds. *Rethinking the Vote: The Politics and Prospects of American Election Reform.* New York: Oxford University Press, 2004.

Feder, Don. "Election Panels 'Fixes' a Disaster." *Boston Globe,* 8 August 2001.

Foner, Eric. *Reconstruction: America's Unfinished Revolution.* New York: HarperCollins, 1988.

"The 43rd President; Text of Supreme Court Ruling in *Bush v. Gore* Florida Recount Case." *New York Times,* 14 December 2000.

Gaziano, Todd, Testimony of. 14 March 2001, http://www.heritage.org/Research/GovernmentReform/Test031401.cfm.

Hanes, Walton. "The Disenfranchisement of the African American Voter in the 2000 Presidential Election: The Silence of the Winner and Loser." *Black Scholar* 31 (2002): 21–4.

Hauserman, Julie. "Jesse Jackson: Florida 'is the Scene of the Crime.'" *Washington Post*, 14 December 2000.

Keyssar, Alexander. *The Right to Vote: The Contested History of Democracy in the United States* New York: Basic Books, 2000.

Lusane, Clarence. *No Easy Victories: Black Americans and the Vote*. New York: Franklin Watts, 1996.

Mintz, John, and Dan Keating. "Florida Ballot Spoilage Likelier For Blacks; Voting Machines, Confusion Cited." *Washington Post*, 3 December 2000.

National Commission on Federal Election Reform. *To Assure Pride and Confidence in the Electoral Process* (August 2001), http://www.tcf.org/Publications/ElectionReform/99_full_report.pdf.

Peréz, C. Lori. "The 2000 Presidential Election, Postelection Contest: A Chronology." *Journal of American History* Web site, http://www.indiana.edu/~jah/election2000/.

Posner, Richard A. *Breaking the Deadlock: The 2000 Election, the Constitution, and the Courts*. Princeton, N.J.: Princeton University Press, 2001.

Raspberry, William. "A Major Waste of Opportunity." *Denver Post*, 3 August 2001.

Sabato, Larry J. *Overtime!: The Election 2000 Thriller*. New York: Longman, 2002.

Samples, John. "Election Reform, Federalism, and the Obligation of Voters." Cato Institute Web site, 23 October 2001, http://www.cato.org/pub_display.php?pub_id=1276.

Walters, Ronald W. *Freedom Is Not Enough: Black Voters, Black Candidates, and American Presidential Politics*. Lanham, Md.: Rowan & Littlefield, 2005.

Videos

CNN. *Election 2000: 36 Days That Gripped the Nation*, 2001. 65 min. An excellent overview of the 2000 election controversy.

The History Channel. *Crossing the Bridge*, 2005. 60 min. A history of the Southern Christian Leadership Conference and its efforts to win black suffrage.

Web Sites

The Advancement Project Web site, http://www.advancementproject.org/.

CNN Election 2000 Web site, http://www.cnn.com/ELECTION/2000/.

National Public Radio Election 2000 Web site, http://www.npr.org/news/national/election2000/#.

INDEX

About the Author

KEVIN D. ROBERTS is Assistant Professor of History at New Mexico State University.